INVISIBLE TO
REMARKABLE

INVISIBLE TO
REMARKABLE

In Today's Job Market,
You Need To Sell Yourself as "Talent",
Not Just Someone Looking For Work.

Discover Why You Need To
Become Your Own Personal Brand.

Copyright © 2012 by Mike Berg, M.Ed.

All rights reserved. No part of this book may be used or reproduced by any means, graphic, electronic, or mechanical, including photocopying, recording, taping or by any information storage retrieval system without the written permission of the publisher except in the case of brief quotations embodied in critical articles and reviews.

iUniverse books may be ordered through booksellers or by contacting:

iUniverse
1663 Liberty Drive
Bloomington, IN 47403
www.iuniverse.com
1-800-Authors (1-800-288-4677)

Because of the dynamic nature of the Internet, any web addresses or links contained in this book may have changed since publication and may no longer be valid. The views expressed in this work are solely those of the author and do not necessarily reflect the views of the publisher, and the publisher hereby disclaims any responsibility for them.

Any people depicted in stock imagery provided by Thinkstock are models, and such images are being used for illustrative purposes only.
Certain stock imagery © Thinkstock.

ISBN: 978-1-4759-1864-9 (sc)
ISBN: 978-1-4759-1865-6 (ebk)

Printed in the United States of America

iUniverse rev. date: 06/28/2012

CONTENTS

1

Begin With The End In Mind

Something happened in the last 3 years. It seemed like overnight, companies started laying off employees and the unemployment rate reached record highs. The news reflected a changing economy and suddenly, the local job market seemed to become a global employment market. For many people, it appeared that the meltdown of home prices and problems in the financial markets appeared to be the temporary reasons for this situation.

However, the financial crisis was actually triggered by a complex combination of valuation and liquidity problems that caused the value of real estate pricing to drop damaging financial institutions globally. Declines in credit availability and declining investor confidence impacted global stock markets, and economies worldwide slowed as credit tightened and international trade declined.

You are about to discover that these changes in the economy are the result of many factors that were bringing us to a new job market several years earlier. Not only has the availability of full-time positions changed, the way people will find and do work is also changing.

The new employment market is not temporary; it's quickly becoming the new world of work. Cost effectiveness, flexible employability, just-in-time production and a global workforce are the new buzzwords in an economy that is now connected globally more than ever. The availability of technology and software for people to connect to the Internet offers almost anyone the chance to become their own company.

Now more than ever, it's not the degree you have, who you know, the school you graduated from, your score on a college entrance exam or how much experience you have, that determines your employment security.

In today's employment market, your success is primarily determined by whether or not you're REMARKABLE. Randomly searching for what's available is no longer a realistic option. Unless you're REMARKABLE, you're invisible.

**You have to begin with the end in mind.
<u>Decide what you want to be</u> and then pursue it.**

This is NOT a book focused on job search. It's transformational thinking to help you understand and apply the concepts of personal branding to become financially independent, be successful in your career, establish yourself as being remarkable and do work that matters.

So how can YOU become remarkable?

It's surprising simple, yet few people know what you are about to discover. Perhaps insights learned from a house fly offer the best perspective.

A True Story

I'm sitting in a quiet room at the Millcroft Inn, a peaceful little place hidden back among the pine trees about an hour out of Toronto. It's just past noon, late July, and I'm listening to the desperate sounds of a life or death struggle going on a few feet away.

There's a small fly burning out the last of its short life's energies in a futile attempt to fly through the glass of the windowpane. The whining wings tell the poignant story of the fly's strategy—try harder. But it's not working.

The frenzied effort offers no hope for survival. Ironically, the struggle is part of the trap. Its determined effort offered no hope for survival. Ironically, its struggle is part of the trap. It is impossible for the fly to try hard enough to succeed at breaking through the glass.

Nevertheless, this little insect has staked its goal through raw effort and determination. This fly is doomed. It will die there on the windowsill.

Across the room, 10 steps away the door is open. Ten seconds of flying time and this small creature could reach the outside world it seeks. With only a fraction of the effort now being wasted, it could be free of this self imposed trap. The breakthrough possibility is there. It would be so easy.

Why doesn't the fly try another approach, something dramatically different? How did it get locked into the idea that this particular route, and determined effort, offers the most promise for success?

What logic is there that in continuing, until death, to seek a breakthrough with "more of the same"? No doubt this approach makes sense to the fly. Regrettably, it's an idea that will kill.

"Trying harder" isn't necessarily the solution to achieving more. It may not offer any real promise for getting what you want in life. Sometimes, in fact, it's a big part of the problem. If you stake your hopes for a breakthrough on trying harder than ever, you may kill your chances of success."

Reprinted with full permission of Pritchett, LP" from the book You² by Price Pritchett, PhD. "all rights reserved." www.pritchettnet.com.

Remember when you were getting ready to graduate from high school? You thought that commencement meant "the end" and you said I'm FREE! Shortly after your graduation party, you probably realized that the word commencement means "to start".

You are about to learn that going forward, your career will no longer be linear with a logical path going from A to B. It's going to zig and zag and probably take 20 different directions throughout your lifetime. Sounds scary doesn't it?

Yet, now more than ever, having a dynamically changing career will allow you to make more money, have more fun and have control of your time. Best of all, YOU will have control of your life and the benefits that come with shaping your own destiny.

Let's begin by taking a look at what's happening in the global employment market to understand how the world of work has changed and how it impacts your ability to compete in the new employment marketplace.

2

What In The World Is Going On?

For the past 20 years, it was the age of the great employer. Success was a stable job at a single company where you worked hard to hopefully go from being a line worker to a position in management.

Then in 2009, a more prominent awareness of the global economy took center stage and we discovered that the world financial situation was in bad shape. Since December of 2007, the economy lost 7 million jobs, taking the unemployment rate to 9.4 percent. The total number of Americans who are currently out of work is estimated to be at 14 million, a 26-year high. Another 9 million find themselves in the category of involuntary part-time workers, a jump of 3.7 million in just 1 year—that's 23 million people in need of full-time work.

Today the national average work week for hourly workers is 33.2 hours, the lowest average work hours in 30 years. A lot of people who thought they had full-time jobs are not getting full-time hours. This trend has been developing over the past 20 years as employers are shifting to "just-in-time" labor. In retail, 20 years ago, 70% of store clerks were full-time, now it's 30%.

Why should you care about what is happening with the global population?

- By 2013 another billion people will have joined an already resource hungry global population.
- More people will need to find work competing in a global employment market.

- Migration will greatly affect the future workplace as people move to search for a better life, better job opportunities, more education, avoid hunger, religious persecution or political instability related to terrorism.
- The United States allows as many as 1 million people a year to start a new life in this country.
- 25% of technology companies in the U.S. were started by foreign born executives and many of them came to the U.S. as children.
- People are also living longer. Adults who are 65 years or older are estimated to increase by 50 percent between 2005 and 2030, putting significant strain on the economy related to healthcare, pensions and the need for supplemental income for adults who lost much of their savings in a declining stock market.
- Factor in an aging population of soon to be retirees, employers will need to replace these workers who in many cases have specialized skills that are not easy to find.
- Older workers are extending their working years to retirement related to a decline in the value of their investment holdings.
- The U.S. Labor Department reported that in mid 2009, on average, there were about 6.3 unemployed workers competing, for each job opening, up from 1.7 workers when the recession began in 2007.
- Today there are over 450 cities worldwide with over 1 million people, each with a massive labor market primarily looking for local employment.

Couple these facts with a global capacity to profitably deliver products and services anywhere in the world, and what was primarily local competition for work, has become a worldwide competitive employment marketplace where employers can find employees at bargain prices.

As a result of these factors and the worldwide financial crisis, the "new" workforce is shaping up to look very different. The good news is that the new world of work offers incredible opportunities to those who embrace it.

Faced with stiffer competition and tighter cash flow, companies are becoming more focused on productivity and bottom-line performance than a candidate's education or qualifications. Competition for jobs is also increasing as management only wants to hire candidates who have clearly identified that they can increase the company's profits, reduce costs or solve a problem.

Different than in the past, employees are now viewed as a variable cost tied to VERIFIABLE performance metrics and an employee will only be kept around if they continue to produce specific results. Companies are already building databases of top talent tied to CRM (Candidate Relationship Management) workflow systems that include advanced workflow design, auto-responders and sophisticated applicant tracking systems. Businesses want a resource list of who they can call when they need someone to deliver specific results.

The era of becoming a personal brand has begun.

The OLD rule—get your resume in front of as many people as you can, hoping that someone needs you and they will give you a call.

The NEW rule—present yourself as "remarkable" by targeting companies that could use your services with clearly defined solutions to help them make money, save money or solve a problem.

Job search technology is changing almost daily with the addition of sophisticated resume scanners and search engines that use advanced algorithms, yet the fundamental rules of business have not changed. In demand skills along with the right relationships and compelling packaging (resumes) are still what determine success in a job search. With so many options and a highly competitive workforce, the winners of today will come from those who have taken the time to make themselves remarkable in a workforce where most job searchers are invisible.

Every day, we read headlines about people losing their jobs. In 2011, over 14 million people were collecting unemployment in the United States. Look carefully at the workplace and you'll see that 2009 was the beginning of an era of a labor market that has become a talent market more than it has ever been. In fact, the new employment market is also becoming more free agent based. The Census Bureau estimates that the U.S. has more than 20 million businesses without paid employees. These small enterprises generate annual revenue totaling almost $1 trillion.

Today inequality in the job market is between those having in demand skills and workers who have essentially become unskilled workers. The new economy has shifted from corporate power to a shift in responsibility and accountability to YOU the individual. The packaging has changed, but ultimately, YOU are your own business, remarkable and marketable because of your TALENT.

The average life expectancy is now approaching 80 and more people are doing knowledge based work. Retiring boomers will constitute a large demographic work force, however in the next 10 years, they will need to be replaced. Look at the work force of today. The birth rate has stabilized relative to the growth of jobs and U.S. labor force statistics indicate that the number of available workers will essentially stop growing in 12 years. We'll need workers, but we won't be able to find them. But understand that the shortage will be in talent workers, not in the general labor force. The bottom line: Workers will essentially be free agents who will need to have talent AND the business savvy to market their services. Translation—you need to be remarkable or you will be invisible! This isn't anything new, however now it's more important than ever.

So what will your new work world look like compared to what it was like just a few years ago?

- You will be self-organized instead of centrally controlled.
- You'll pick up your proposal at FedEx then meet a client at Starbucks. You'll FedEx a revised contract for your client on the way home.
- You will use an e-commerce merchant account like PayPal to get paid over the Internet and let QuickBooks record the transaction automatically.
- Later in the month you'll email your accounting files to an accountant (who you may never meet face-to-face) and get a company financial report as a PDF the next day.

Yes, the world of work has drastically changed and these are tough times for everybody. But let's not lose sight of the benefits and the good things that will come about because of these trends. In good times, people leap into talent based self employment; in bad times, they get pushed. Ask most people why they don't work on their own and they'll respond, "I need to keep my job for the health insurance benefits". How would their attitude change if they knew that Costco can likely offer them an individual health care plan for less than they are paying through their current employer?

Keep in mind that the message I'm sharing with you is NOT that you should become self employed. You can still work for a company as an employee, but you need to have a secondary source of income. The key point is that ultimately, you need to become a free agent worker who has multiple sources of income from many clients. Then if your current employer no longer needs your services, you still have an income as a back-up. Keep in mind that YOU are the CEO (Chief Executive Officer) of your life whether you run your own business or work within a company.

Free Agent Employment is actually how most businesses throughout history have operated. Today, around 60% of enterprises in the world are family or small businesses. In fact 80% of business transactions in the worldwide are still made with cash! It's hard to believe but it's true. Travel internationally and you will understand how this is reality. The industrial economy separated work and family. A free-agent economy is bringing them back together.

Much has changed because of the Internet. Wireless access and Internet hotspots are standard parts of the daily business experience. Instant messaging, social networking, Twitter, Facebook and other communication tools are now reliable and simple enough to completely override the "corporate infrastructure" of the past. Online services of every conceivable form are available to make it easier to manage business from almost anywhere, and all of these resources can be fully utilized without requiring that a person sit in a specific office. Think about it. Make a reservation on Jet Blue Airlines and you will likely talk to home based retirees who are all located in one state.

Today's worker is quickly becoming "always on and always accessible". You log in, you're authenticated, you can do what you're authorized to do, your information is logged and you move on to the next task of the day. The days of sitting in an office and being paid for your time are coming to an end for most workers. Look at the statistics and you'll see a rapidly changing workforce and the way people do business.

- 8.3 million are independent contractors.
- 2.3 million work through temporary agencies.
- Fewer than 1 in 10 work for a Fortune 500 company.
- Self employed contractors represent 16% of the workforce—by 2020 that number is expected to be 50%.

What's driving this? More companies are engaging talent on a contract basis to solve short-term needs and engaging specialists for project work. There are fewer jobs for available workers. In many major metropolitan areas, there are 5 candidates for every open position and that number is growing—a Wal-Mart in a small city had 3000 people show up for 300 jobs!

People are gradually discovering that it can be more fulfilling to work for 5 clients than it is to work for 1 boss and it's much safer in terms of financial security. Technology tools have made working without boundaries easy. With the proliferation of inexpensive computers, wireless handheld devices and low-cost connections to the Internet, you can now own the means of production AND product delivery.

The organization person is history. Taking their place is America's new economic icon: the "free agent"—the job-hopping, tech-savvy, fulfillment-seeking, self-reliant and independent worker. Already 30 million strong, they are transforming America in ways that are profound and exciting. The concept of co-worker has changed to "co-working". Like Windows or Linux on computers, the Free Agent Work Force establishes the platform on which the free agent economy operates. Its basic unit is trust tied to a personal relationship, not just a company. You now have a global communications network as your platform for finding and delivering a product or a service.

Over the years, companies have gotten leaner as employees have gotten more productive. And they won't rehire as much when times improve because they'll want to keep their profit margins high. The age of big business supporting thousands of workers is coming to a close. Any way you look at it, these are challenging times we live in. Starting a company is a risky proposition. But this is one time when looking for a long-term job with benefits might be riskier.

Look for sustainable employment with jobs that will give you an ongoing living. Don't wait until you come up with the perfect idea. Take action now. You'll be better off if you work out the kinks as you face them. Just get started.

Talent isn't the next big thing, it's the only thing.

In this new era of employment, you'll need to do 3 things to survive.

1. Identify your MARKETABLE talent.
2. Have a SYSTEM that utilizes technology to build business relationships to market your talent.
3. SELL your skills or products tied to measurable metrics that can make money, solve a problem or reduce costs for your customers.

Employment demographics over the past 5 years reveal that organizational workers are being replaced by employees who think like free agents. You may think that the lack of jobs is primarily a result of our struggling economy. But the shift in the labor force away from traditional full-time jobs toward contract work didn't start with this recession. The job market downturn that began 2 years ago has just accelerated the transformation to the contract, project based workforce that is becoming the new world of work.

Cost cutting and restructuring became wide spread when the media showed us a global marketplace that was living beyond their means using credit to keep things running. It sounded simple. Companies simply needed to reduce costs and become more efficient to get their finances in order. We were told that we are in a recession and although it would take some time, things would be back to normal if we were patient. Since then, we've all been waiting for the job engine to restart as it usually does following a recession. But small businesses, the group that generally leads the creation of jobs, aren't hiring like we expected.

It's easy to blame the economy for a weak job market, but a cross correlation of labor and business statistics identifies the real cause of rising unemployment globally. The traditional business labor model doesn't apply anymore, primarily due to technology and an increasingly globalized employment market.

Essentially was has evolved is a contingent, freelance economy where businesses are electing to hire on an "as-needed" basis, relying on a contract workforce who have developed a business of working on projects with multiple employers instead of working full-time with one company. Part-time and full-time contract workers are estimated to make up 25% of the current U.S. work force. In the past 4 years, companies have increased their outsourcing by 25%.

The new employment marketplace mindset is not HAVING a job but DOING a job. In many cases, full-time corporate workers who have a job also do a job to supplement their income. A common example of this is a school teacher who is also an on-line instructor who runs an on-line e-commerce training business from a home office.

Many employers need help, but they can't afford to hire on-site employees. It's estimated that providing an office workspace for an employee costs a company an average $10,000 a year. Step back from the day-to-day media reports of a bad economy and take a look at the NEW economy and what you need to do if you want to be a player in the new game of stable employment.

Key to this change in the employer-employee work model is our ability to collaborate on-line with virtually anybody that has access to an Internet connection. The Internet and its numerous free tools to connect globally, now offer almost any individual the marketplace, platform and infrastructure to support their own business. Affordable customer relationship management (CRM) software, the ability to collect payments securely on-line and a global reach to connect with customers through social networks, has leveled the playing field for anyone willing to build and monetize their personal brand. We were isolated, now we're connected. The typical individual didn't have the time, the money or the connections to operate as a free agent just a few years ago.

Now they can. Now YOU can at almost zero cost!

In the past, companies were required to invest in developing talent from an internal work force to be successful. Now many employers want to buy what they need, when they need it. Hiring today is becoming an on-demand, project based relationship. Is this the future of work? It seems likely. Employers today are shifting to a blended workforce using full-time and contingent workers. We now live in a project economy and this employer-contractor model is where to look for employment security. In a highly competitive and volatile global economy, companies need a workforce they can switch on and off as needed.

Today, about 30% of the U.S. job market, roughly 42 million workers, is made up of independent contractors and part-time or temporary staff. This trend is also expected to spread beyond traditional contracted jobs to professions like accounting, engineering, health care, law and sales.

We are now in the early stages of what will be a project based work-place where workers will need to structure their career around a project SERVICES model instead of an ORGANIZATION based full-time job within a corporation. The Internet has made local jobs global opportunities for anyone that can get on line. It's time to stop and ask yourself, "How does the new "Internet Connected" global job market affect me?"

3

It's a Small World After All

In the new plug-n-play world, what happens in other countries has more impact than you might think. The world's population has tripled in the past 70 years with most of the growth coming from outside the United States. Meanwhile, faster rates of economic growth, particularly in Asia, have accelerated job creation outpacing the growth of the available labor force. Lower birth rates, higher levels of education and higher rates of economic growth are gradually restoring the balance between population and employment opportunities globally.

The world is also in the early stages of another demographic revolution that will have a significant impact on the future of employment worldwide—a steep decline in the birth rate and an increase in life expectancy in economically advanced countries.

The result of these trends will be a reduction in the number of young people entering the job market and a surge in the size of the elderly population. 50% of the population in industrialized countries are now in the dependent age groups, which include those under 15 and those over 65. As the old age population grows, the working age population will shrink even more. By 2013, it's estimated that the labor-force growth in the U.S. will be almost zero resulting in a shortage of 17 million working age people by 2020. China will be short 15 million and India is expected to have a surplus of 45 million workers.

Another trend that has been developing for years is finally starting to create serious problems. It's not a shortage of jobs; it's the lack of skilled workers. Basic labor, non skilled manufacturing jobs are being exported to lower wage developing countries. At the same time, the demand for workers with higher levels of technical knowledge has been rising rapidly. Consequently there is less demand for workers who have not continued to upgrade their knowledge and skills. Rising skill requirements combined with a shortage of skills is creating a growing disparity between the skills of the workforce and the needs of the economy. Numerous studies confirm the existence of a substantial shortage of workers with the required level of skills to fill vacant positions. The technical skills shortage applies to jobs in almost every sector. Even in India, which produces 400,000 engineers annually, corporations are finding it increasingly difficult to find qualified workers.

An aging global population is also a factor. The proportion of adults over 60 in high-income countries is expected to increase from 8% to 19% by 2050, while the number of children being born will drop by one third. The aging of the population is leading to labor shortages, skills shortages and an increased tax burden on the working population in order to support social security income for the increasing retired population.

Migration is also increasing between industrialized countries as well as from developing to industrialized countries. Outsourcing began with the migration of manufacturing jobs to lower wage developing countries. With the increasing business transactions tied to the Internet, manufacturing positions have declined and now represent less than 25% of jobs globally. Service and knowledge industry employment have become 85% of employment in most countries. This trend is also accompanied by a major expansion of temporary and part-time positions resulting from companies trying to maintain a flexible work team to hedge against fluctuations in the economy.

Just like the Disney song, "It's a Small World After All", we are seeing that we truly are part of a global family. It's actually nothing new. The Internet is showing us a connected world that has really been there all the time. If you shift your focus from locally available jobs to what's in demand globally, you'll get a better picture of how the world employment market affects you.

4

A Coca Cola Employment Market

Why does the US unemployment rate seem to stay about the same despite news that companies are hiring? Companies are hiring but the real hiring is mostly overseas, Look at corporate hiring nationwide and you'll see that the era of a global workforce is rapidly emerging. International employment markets are growing twice as fast as they are domestically.

Take a look at the latest labor statistics and you'll see that many U.S. jobs have been moving overseas in the last 10 years. In the past, clothes and commodity items were the primary goods made more cheaply overseas. Now the products are software and high technology electronics.

Look at GNP data and you'll also see that the products being made overseas are primarily being sold to the emerging markets of China, Brazil and India, not in the U.S. Think about it. The # 1 English speaking country in the world is China! The reality of the new economy is that U.S. companies are going where there is product demand with more attractive profit margins. Asia-Pacific sales soared 40% in the first nine months of 2011, compared with 17% in the United States. 50% of corporate revenue in the S&P 500 in the last 2 years has primarily come from outside the United States.

China is now the world's 2nd largest economy and on their way to becoming # 1. Major global companies are now focusing on the geography where they sell their products and tailoring products to meet local customer needs.

A key factor behind this runaway international growth is the rise of the middle class in emerging countries. By 2015, it's estimated the number of consumers in Asia's middle class will equal those in Europe and North

America combined. Most of the growth over the next 10 years is happening in Asia. The current CEO of Coca-Cola estimates that a billion consumers will enter the middle class in the next 10 years, primarily in Africa, China and India. Coke is aggressively targeting those markets and now only 13% of Coke's 93,000 global employees are in the U.S.

So where does this mean to you as part of the U.S. employment market? Begin to reinvent yourself to compete in a global market and get to know how the global marketplace can offer you access to new customers (employers) beyond your local employment market.

- Consider developing an in-demand product or service that can be digitally distributed in the U.S.
- Make what you offer REMARKABLE—become a specialist in something.
- Understand that your income will almost always be in direct proportion to the number of people you serve.
- Use the Internet to help more people get what they want.
- Understand the latest technologies for e-commerce—Musion developed a 3-D holographic projection system that Cisco Systems used to "beam" a couple of its executives onstage to deliver a speech. That was over 4 years ago. You need to be aware of the current technology tools available to you.

Where are you in understanding how to use technology and your skills to help people and businesses make money, save money or solve a problem? It's key to your employment security.

The secret to transforming yourself to be successful in generating income in the new job market is to stop focusing on finding a full-time job with benefits as your employment goal. Target ways you can help many people (employers) get what they want, recognizing that YOUR INCOME WILL ALMOST ALWAYS BE IN DIRECT PROPORTION TO THE NUMBER OF PEOPLE YOU SERVE.

5

It's Time to "Bounce"

You don't necessarily need a big paying job to become a success. I think too many people are only focused on finding a full-time, high paying job as their sole source of income. The new economy requires a different way of thinking. The reality is that the world of work has changed and the past ways of doing things for the most part are not coming back.

> Wal-Mart closed 10 Sam's Club stores and terminated 11,200 Sam's Club employees after switching to a private company to provide in-store product demonstrations instead of using their own employees.

> 7,500 people turned in applications for 350 jobs at a Wal-Mart Supercenter.

The daily headlines reflect the same message. Employers are doing more with less and hiring who they need and only when they need them. Perhaps this job search mindset needs to be your new way of thinking.

- **It's time to let go**—waiting for the former job market to come back, may delay your actions to take a different path where success is more realistically possible.
- **Most careers are no longer linear and don't involve one employer.** Consider developing multiple sources of income, including some residual income to truly give yourself economic security.
- **Try a "Stepping Stone Approach"**—Make minor changes each week to achieve short-term goals. Small successes will give you

renewed confidence and protect you from investing too much time in long term goals that may be unachievable.

- **Strive for Daily Incremental Achievement**—Focus on one thing at a time. Realize that in many cases, multitasking may actually reduce your productivity by 50%.
- **Avoid "Analysis Paralysis"—Stop analyzing**. Don't wait for the "perfect moment" when you think you have considered every angle. Take action with reasonable preparation and adjust your plan as you go.

How should you cope with the new employment market?

It's time to "bounce". Position yourself for success by bouncing from one success to another where you use the lessons learned from achieving (or failing to achieve) one short term goal to get to the next one. Today, job search or personal brand development requires a different kind of thinking. Don't get caught up in what's worked in the past. If you rely on past data (often times outdated) to drive your decisions, you may end up with variations of past results that may be just incremental improvements and never produce significant results.

A great example of this is Simon Cowell, an American Idol judge. He went bankrupt, lost a million dollars and had to move back in with his parents. Years later Cowell earned $40 million per season on American Idol and eventually sold half of his S Records to BMG for $43 million.

He started his career at EMI Music Publishing, where he worked his way up from the assistant to an A&R representative to a record producer, but in the early '80s, he left the company to create his own label, E&S Music. The company went bankrupt, and Cowell returned to EMI. Then he tried to launch his own label again in 1985 with Fanfare Records, which enjoyed more success but was forced to fold when its parent company went under. Frustrated by his second major setback, Cowell began working as an A&R consultant for BMG, where he found success producing novelty records by stars from other areas of the entertainment industry. He signed a number of successful bands to the label, and began working on other music-based projects like the British show Pop Idol, which would be reincarnated in the US as American Idol. The rest is history.

How can you repackage or reinvent yourself?

What can you do where you can charge $100 and help a 1000 people get what they need? (That's $100,000 a year)

When Proctor & Gamble (P&G) launched Pampers as a disposable diaper, the product was revolutionary. Years later, "Pampers Cruisers" was just incremental progress—nothing more than a small gain in market share and nothing revolutionary.

Yet Tide2Go, a stain removal pen you can keep in your desk was a radical innovation for P&G. A simple product that focused on solving a consumer need in a more convenient way.

The best ideas often come from your day to day experience. They evolve by keeping your eyes open and truly analyzing the world around you. If you are looking for a job or changing your career track, ask yourself, "How can I do something more than just posting my resume on-line and applying to jobs hoping for a call-back?"

Remember the "It's Time to Think Different" television ad? It was the advertising slogan tied to a TV commercial created for Apple in 1982. It featured black and white video footage of significant historical people—Albert Einstein, Bob Dylan, Martin Luther King, Jr., Richard Branson, John Lennon, Thomas Edison, Muhammad Ali, Ted Turner, Mahatma Gandhi and Pablo Picasso. The commercial ends with an image of a young girl opening her closed eyes, as if to see the possibilities before her.

Revitalize Your Job Search By Focusing On Getting What You Want Not Just What's Available On A Job Board.

Once you know what you want, the job search process and your desire for a meaningful career will take on a new perspective.

Since defining what you can offer and doing things that get results needs to be reality based, you'll need to carefully manage the steps you take to get where you want to go. Let's take a look at how it's the "little things" that often make the biggest differences in what we have to do to get where we want to go.

6

Why UPS Trucks Always Turn Right

The UPS package delivery system uses packages marked with special codes to load the trucks by address as well as a delivery sequence to make as many right turns as possible. Turning left usually requires waiting for oncoming traffic and traffic lights, so by eliminating that idle time, UPS saves millions of dollars.

Since the trucks are driven an average of 2.5 billion miles a year, their package flow software combined with right-turn only planning, eliminates 29 million miles of driving and saves 3 million gallons of fuel annually. Efficiency is so much of a focus at UPS, that at the end of the day, their brown trucks are parked 5 inches apart with their rear view mirrors overlapping to maximize parking space. Using advanced analytics, UPS discovered relationships in their truck usage data that highlighted how minor changes could produce amazing results! But look closely and you'll see that there is more than just a lesson in cost savings here.

The real insight is that "If you can't measure it, you can't manage it." Many people carefully plan a vacation but passively manage how they will develop their career. Too often they wait for a layoff or job dissatisfaction to motivate them to start a new career track. Periodically evaluate what results you are getting tied to what you are doing. Set up a simple spreadsheet and "know your numbers". Then decide how you can improve your results.

Your "numbers" spreadsheet needs to define what work you are doing related to the results (income) you earn.

Several years ago, I was at a party and met a guy who worked as a Manager for a restaurant. He asked me what he could do to earn more money.

He told me he earned a salary of $40,000 a year with just a high school education. Using the concept of "knowing your numbers", we defined the hours he worked per week and calculated his hourly rate at 8.00 an hour. He was shocked. After adding up his common 10 hour a day work schedule, the nights he was called in for employees who called in sick and weekend/holiday work, his hourly pay rate made him realize that he was significantly underpaid. Just knowing his true hourly rate motivated him to think differently about his career and what he needed to do to increase his income.

His wife ran a part-time catering business where she earned $30,000 a year but worked half as much as her husband. Perhaps he should work with her to expand the catering business and potentially double his income. Measuring your results is the secret to managing your career. Once you know your rate of return, it's easier to decide where you need to invest your time.

Studies have shown that more often than not, 80% of your success comes from 20% of your efforts. Just think of how much more productive you could be if you focused 80% of your effort on 20% of the things that get you the best results! The secret is to know what those "20% activities" are.

Start today to measure your activities and track the results. If sending out resumes for jobs listed on job boards gets you a 4% response rate but 60% of your interviews come from networking events, where should you focus your efforts? For many job searchers, they rarely get calls for jobs posted on job boards, yet they spend 90% of their time sending out more resumes. Try a mix of search strategies and see what works for you. Over the course of a month, a minor change in your job search focus can produce amazingly different results. Track your results tied to what you are doing and the data may surprise you.

In the movie Jerry McGuire starring Tom Cruise, actor Cuba Gooding, Jr. made famous the phrase "Show Me the Money". Years later, a variation of that saying, "Show Me Results" is what's on the mind of most hiring managers. Looking for a job or getting new customers is a job. Measure what you do and manage your activities tied to what gets results. If you are turning left instead of right, you may be too late to pick up a package that's being returned to the sender because nobody's home. Paying attention to the details is important, but you need to focus on the right work force model. The model has changed for most people, yet few of them understand what those changes are.

Let's take a look at the traditional employer-employee model that most job searchers are still looking for and an alternative that may be the answer to your long-term employment security.

7

Become a Hunter AND a Farmer

For most people, their job is sitting at a desk for 8 hours a day and essentially trading their time for money. Ask most people what they earn and they respond in terms of how much they make per hour.

Having a full-time job seems to be the goal of most people who ultimately want to be assured of a steady income in return for showing up on a regular basis to complete tasks assigned by their employer.

Take a closer look at the changing world of work, and you'll see an evolving trend toward DOING versus having a job. Understanding this difference is the key to your future success, regardless of your chosen profession.

A simple analogy to understand this shift in the job market is thinking of yourself as either a hunter or a farmer. A hunter goes after business opportunities and the farmer takes care of the business. Most corporate workers are farmers and most sales people are the hunters who find the business. To survive in today's employment market, you need to become a hunter AND a farmer. You can no longer rely on one corporation to produce opportunities for you to work. You need to have multiple companies (clients) that hire you to do what they need done.

Since the Internet now offers most of us the opportunity to have customers almost anywhere, we can control our income by increasing the number of people we help and by offering a valuable product or service.

Notice that the focus is on having "customers" (many employers) not just "renting" your time to one employer. Let me remind you that, **your**

income will almost always be in direct proportion to the number of people you serve.

Decide on what you can offer that is in demand and then spilt your time between finding new customers and delivering a great product or service. Change your thinking to DOING versus HAVING a job and you will become more marketable AND employable.

Today there are fewer opportunities to be employed, so focus on developing yourself as a "brand" and market what makes you remarkable. Then ask yourself, "How you can serve more people?"

The more people you help get what they want, the more you'll get what you want. If you're currently unemployed, consider spending 50% of your time job hunting. Use the other 50% to create a business for yourself. Explore what you can do that is marketable, can be delivered digitally and is in demand by a large number of people. Get good at finding customers and offering something that is remarkable.

Most of the workforce today has been raised with the mindset that the best way to earn a living is to have a job. For most of us, when we graduated from high school or college, we assumed it's time to go out and get a job. But like many things the masses do, it doesn't mean it's the best option, particularly in today's employment market. In fact, getting "a job" may NOT be your best option. We all get used to doing things a certain way, but that way may not always be what's best for us. It pays to step back now and then get some perspective. Ask yourself the Dr. Phil question, "How's that working for you?" If you are working and don't see a clear path to a stable income or if you are unemployed and can't seem to find a job, it's time to change your thoughts to change your world. So often it's when we drastically change our thinking about how we approach a problem that we get amazing results.

Most people focus on the EFFORT they put into accomplishing a task instead of the RESULTS they generate. By focusing on results, you can transform your "employability mindset" in less than an hour. The new employment marketplace requires you to find customers (employers) and do work (projects) for a variety of employers (customers). Ultimately this will ensure your employability and income security.

Using the hunter and farmer analogy, we join a company to keep it going by performing a specialized task like being a farmer focused on keeping an existing business going with little concern for getting customers to support the business. Unless we are in sales, our focus is likely task oriented where we get paid for our time to complete projects. The new corporate marketplace is rapidly changing to hiring farmers to do specialized tasks and then send them home when their project is completed. Essentially, it's now becoming your responsibility to get customer's as a "hunter" so you can do the "farming" for multiple employers.

You already have the leverage to make a difference, the technology to spread your ideas and the power to build your own personal brand. At first glance this appears to be very unpredictable and an insecure way of working, yet in reality, it's the best model for ensuring your employment security and maximizing your income.

Still not convinced? Consider this:

- **Having a "Job" Is Essentially Trading Your Time for Money**—Because you only get paid when you're working, you are essentially "renting" yourself and trading income for time. The key is to separate your value from your time by either adding a way to increase your income with an added commission or some payment based on results, not just time.
- **Limited Experience**—A job only gives you experience at THAT job. You might think it's important to get a job to gain experience. But if your skills ever become obsolete, then your experience won't be worth much. Ask yourself, "What will the experience you're gaining right now be worth in 3 years?" Will your job even exist or be in demand in the next 3 years?
- **Employment Security**—Many employees believe getting a job is the safest and most secure way to support themselves. Look at the increasing number of layoffs and contractors in the workforce along with the amount of work being outsourced to other countries. Does having only one source of income truly give you

employment security? Could your job be digitally outsourced to workers on the Internet? (Think of on-line university classes and buying books from Amazon instead of a local bookstore).

- **The Value of Relationships**—many people find that their jobs are their primary social outlet. They hang out with the same people working in the same field. Yet relationships are the key to get a job and increase your value to others in the business world. Today, it's what you know AND who knows you that counts. Working for one company can limit your exposure to develop new relationships.
- **Getting A "Job" Versus Doing A Job**—realize that you want to earn income by providing value, not just offering your time. You can apply this concept working with an employer or by starting your own business in addition to working for a company. The key is to find a way to have multiple streams of income along with one that offers residual income.

Stop looking for a job and focus on providing valuable services and employers and customers will be calling YOU for work.

8

A Money Market Career

Most people know that the riskiest financial strategy is to have all of your money in one stock. Yet for most working people, they have all of their income dependent on one company. Think about it. If you lose your income, almost everything else in your life will be affected. Why then should you entrust your financial security to one company or one career.

In this new employment market, you need a career that includes diversified sources of income along with one that includes a residual income component. Consider these options:

- An eBay business where you can sell an on-line product that adds extra part-time income.
- A part-time job where you teach a night class.
- Work weekends doing a job that offers a secondary cash flow that can teach you new skills.
- Write a book where you can earn residual income—you do the work once but keep earning money over time.
- Set up affiliate marketing links on a Blog to earn referral income automatically.

Now more than ever, the Internet offers most of these options for little, if any investment, other than your time. Think of your career as an income portfolio instead of tasks that you do. Track the results you get for your effort and focus on what earns you the best return for your time.

Focus on Cash Flow instead of a Salary—Careers today are moving away from the traditional 40-hour work week to more self-directed opportunities for generating income. The jobs of the future are becoming project based and tied to multiple employers who need your services periodically.

Know Your Rate of Return—There are often different ways to achieve the same career goal. Some ways may take less time but produce the same result. Calculate your rate/hour and try to maximize what you earn for what you do. If you earn 100K but have to work 70 hours per week you're only earning $27.47 / hour. Use your time more effectively and you could work less and earn more per hour.

Manage Risk—Find a mix of income opportunities that align with your talents to minimize risk and the stress of trying to start something outside your area of expertise. Think of ways your income sources can complement each other.

Invest in Yourself—For most people, training stops when they graduate from school. Invest in yourself by setting aside time and money to use for continuing education to stay current in your field and learn new things that may make you more valuable.

Let's take a look at why focusing on what you WANT is far better than focusing on what you have DONE.

9

Your Past Is Not Your Future

When Joanne Kathleen (J.K.) Rowling wrote the first paragraph of a book that would grow into the multibillion-dollar Harry Potter franchise, she was a nearly broke and a single mother struggling with depression.

The first manuscript was rejected by 12 publishers before a small London publishing house decided to print it. The initial print run was 1,000 copies, half of which went to libraries. After a number of rejections, she finally sold the book, Harry Potter and the Sorcerer" for publication in the U.S. for about $4,000. But Rowling decided to write and sell a few more books. She is now wealthier than the Queen of England.

As a single mother living in Scotland, Rowling became an international literary sensation in 1999, when the first three installments of her Harry Potter children's book series took over the top three slots of The New York Times best-seller list. The phenomenal response to Rowling's books culminated in July 2000, when the fourth volume in the series, Harry Potter and the Goblet of Fire, became the fastest-selling book in literary history.

By the summer of 2000, the first three Harry Potter books, Harry Potter and the Sorcerer's Stone, Harry Potter and the Chamber of Secrets and Harry Potter and the Prisoner of Azkaban earned approximately $480 million in three years, with over 35 million copies printed in 35 languages. Potter and the Half Blood Prince, sold 6.9 million copies in the United States in its first 24 hours, it was the biggest opening in publishing history. A film version of Harry Potter and the Sorcerer's Stone, was released in 2001.

In its opening weekend in the U.S., the film was shown on a record 8,200 screens earning an estimated $93.5 million ($20 million more than the previous record holder, the1999 movie The Lost World: Jurassic Park).

This is not just another success story. It's a real world example of why your past (good or bad) is not your future. I often hear people say, I used to make 90K a year and now look at me. Life will never be the same after I was laid off.

Now more than ever, life is NEVER going to be the same. Changes in technology and the evolution of a global employment and product distribution market have made reinventing yourself a key component to ensure your future employability. The phrase "I need to find a job" needs to be changed to, "What product or service can I offer that is in demand". Age, location and education, more often than not, have no real predictable impact on where you'll end up.

- The current CEO of Ford Motor Company started at Ford when he was 72—most people retire at age 65.
- Lady Gaga released "The Fame" in 2008—within 4 years, her net worth was $90 million.
- Mark Zuckerberg launched Facebook from his college dormitory room in 2004 when he was 20—six years later his net worth is over $7 billion—he never graduated from college.

What is your plan? Do you have a plan? What is it that you can offer that is in demand and how will you deliver it?

Think about who are the most successful people in our world today? Most of them are self employed and have their own personal brand. Your brand should be focused on the goal of branding yourself as a celebrity within your market. You don't need to become a Hollywood superstar, you just need to become the go-to-person in your field and within your market. You need to brand yourself as an expert AND as a *remarkable* person. It's not good enough simply to be considered good at what you do; you also need to be memorable. You need to be foremost in the minds of potential clients, so that when they need your services or products, you are the first person they think of.

Becoming a personal brand doesn't mean transforming yourself into a totally different person. It means getting really good at one thing. But getting good at something doesn't help you if nobody knows about it. Who are you, and what are you good at? What skills or knowledge sets you apart from your competition? Your brand should position you as an expert in your field and it should reflect the specialized skills or knowledge that your competition doesn't have, or doesn't communicate. You also need to do work that matters. Ask yourself, "What's in demand and what can I offer that is of value to large numbers of people".

Welcome to the era of personal branding where almost any profession can offer you a chance to become your own personal brand. Social networking made possible by the Internet now offers you the opportunity to compete just like a large corporation.

The power of the Internet offers you the chance of a lifetime if you are willing to focus your thoughts and use the power of relationships to reach your goals!

10

Chance Favors the Prepared Mind

So often when you talk to someone looking for work, you hear them mention that they are hoping to get a "lucky break". Yet more often than not, 99% of successful people didn't have a single big break, even if they point to one. In reality, it's what people do bit by bit that turns their struggle into a success story. Getting on American Idol is often seen as someone's lucky break, yet if you research contestant's paths to getting there, you'll see it's the result of many failures that finally resulted in success. Big breaks come from putting yourself in a favorable position with hard work, networking and passion. Consider these examples of celebrities who found their "lucky break".

Harrison Ford

While Ford dabbled in acting in the 1960s, he also took up carpentry, earning more as a woodworker to the stars than he did playing bit parts in television shows. During that time, he gathered mentors, one of whom eventually led him to George Lucas, who chose him for a part in the 1973 film, American Graffiti. Lucky for him, both Christopher Walken and Al Pacino turned Lucas down when presented with the role of Hans Solo in the 1977 mega-hit, Star Wars.

Madonna

The former Madonna Ciconne of Michigan suffered through stints at Dunkin Donuts, a coat-checker at the Russian Tea Room and as a model on her way to a career in music and dance. Her first big break came when she got a demo tape to well-connected DJ Mark Kamin in New York City.

Kamin passed the tracks along to Seymour Stein of Sire Records, who ultimately marketed Madonna under his label.

Jon Stewart

Voted "Best Sense of Humor" by his high school graduating class in Lawrenceville, N.J., a directionless Jonathan Stuart Leibowitz logged time after college as a construction worker, busboy, assistant high-school soccer coach and puppeteer for disabled children before mustering the confidence to move to New York. There, he made his stand-up debut at The Bitter End comedy club. After a few movie acting stints, Stewart went on to become a fake-news legend as host of Comedy Central's The Daily Show where he earns an estimated $14 million a year.

Brad Pitt

Just two credits shy of a college degree from the University of Missouri, Brad headed to Los Angeles where he worked odd jobs (including a stint at an El Pollo Loco chicken fast food restaurant) to make ends meet. Understanding that good looks and effort only get you so far in the movie business, Pitt hooked up with renowned acting coach Roy London. Among his fellow students was Patrick Swayze. That move (and thousands of sit-ups) paid off. For the last 10 years, Pitt has routinely earned between $10 million and $30 million per film.

Susan Boyle

Everyone knows reality shows can change one lucky performer's life. But Scottish singer Susan Boyle discovered something more powerful—her plain appearance and lack of professional training wasn't a handicap. When she belted out "I Dreamed a Dream" from Les Miserables on Britain's Got Talent in April 2009, the audience gave her a standing ovation and the audition video quickly became a YouTube sensation. Boyle's first album was one of the bestselling debut albums by a female artist in 20 years.

David Letterman

The late-night funnyman broke into the business with a flop. After a string of guest appearances on comedy shows, sitcoms and game shows, Letterman landed a hosting gig for a TV pilot called The Riddlers. The series was a bust, but Letterman got noticed by the producers of The Tonight Show with Johnny Carson. He soon became a regular guest, and eventually became a TV talk show host who earns an estimated $40 million a year.

Steven Spielberg

The film great has been making movies (and money) since he was kid, when he charged a 25-cent admission fee to attend a screening. While attending California State University in Long Beach, Spielberg made his first short film, a 24 minute film called Amblin. After Sidney Sheinberg, then a vice president of production for Universal's TV business saw the film, he signed Spielberg to a long-term contract. Thanks in part to the 2009 Indiana Jones movie, of which he split a large portion of the back-end receipts with George Lucas and actor Harrison Ford, Spielberg brought home $150 million in one year.

Recognizing the power of your thoughts and how little things can add up to make a big difference, let's take a look at how drinking coffee can offer you some insights about the way you should think about becoming remarkable.

11

The Connection between Coffee and Success

Think about the brand of coffee that you were drinking 5 years ago. More than likely, it was a well known brand advertised on TV priced at $4.29 a pound. Then along came Starbucks where you went with your friends to socialize. The coffee was more expensive but you decided that the experience was worth the price.

Eventually Starbucks started selling their coffee in grocery stores and one day you saw it on sale for $6.29/lb. You bought a bag and enjoyed 2 weeks of premium coffee at your home. Then a bag went back up to the regular $8.95/lb. and you had to decide—continue with a cup of Starbucks or go back to your value brand?

A premium brand coffee was your new standard—time for an upgrade. Notice how your buying decisions were small enough that you were able to update your standard of coffee one small step at a time without really thinking about it. Issues related to cost or your need to save money probably never came into your mind. And once you started drinking the premium coffee, you essentially decided that you would never go back to a value brand. Somehow you found a way to adjust your buying options to enjoy the taste of a cup of Starbucks. The gap between what you wanted and what you settled for was small enough to allow you to upgrade without having to make any radical changes. Little upgrades became your new standard and a better standard.

Amazing success for most people almost never happens when they try to make changes that are too big. Once you decide what you want, do something each DAY that gets you closer to your goal. One day you start a blog, then you start getting ideas to write a book and then before you know it, you are planning a speaking tour reaching out to people directly to help them reach their goals. Realize that SMALL steps to reach your goals are the secret.

Drinking premium coffee offers another insight. Once you tasted a great cup of coffee, it's unlikely you will go back to a value brand.

As you improve your standard of living as a result of reaching your goals, you are essentially preparing yourself to resist regressing back to where you were when you started. A Starbucks competitor used a great marketing slogan in the 1990's, "Life's too short to drink lousy coffee!" The implied message is still valid.

Decide TODAY what you want out of your life and more specifically your career. Then write down the steps to get there starting with simple DAILY goals that will become something AMAZING in the next 6 to 12 months. The next time you're sipping a cup of coffee, realize that Starbucks has 17,009 stores in 50 countries, including 11,000 in the US, 1000 in Canada and 700 in the United Kingdom. Starbucks was founded in 1971 by an English teacher, a history teacher and a writer. Last year the company generated $10 billion in revenue. Not bad for a goal of selling a cup of coffee to one customer at a time.

For many people, their focus on success is related to their income as it relates to an annual salary. In the new employment market, you need to change your focus to cash-flow and multiple income streams to truly have economic security. With your new focus on becoming a farmer AND a hunter, let's take a look at simple economics can make contract work a better option than what you have now or what you think you want to find in a typical job.

12

The Dog Theory of Income

The median annual household income in the US is $49,000.

How much did you earn last year? For many people, they think that a degree or specialized knowledge is the key to making more money. It's true that brain surgeons make more money than baby sitters but it's also possible to be a professional dog walker and make more money than a desktop computer technician with a degree. Let's do the math with a target hourly rate of $15.

$15 x 12 dogs = $180 per day (you could walk 3 dogs at a time and work 4 times a day for 1 hour)
$180 day x 5 days = $900 a week
$900 x 4 weeks = $3600 a month
$3600 month x 12 = $43,200 a year

Look carefully and you will discover 2 amazing things about earning money.

1. **Your income will be in direct proportion to the number of people you serve.**

If a little money from a lot of people doesn't work for you, consider what you can offer that is valuable enough to charge a premium price so you can sell less but make more per sale. Lamborghini produces an average of only 4000 exotic cars a year—a 2011 model sells for $237,600!

2. **The level of service or the exclusivity of what you have to offer will determine how much you can charge**.

As you adapt to the changing job market, ask yourself, "How can I serve more people AND increase the level of my service or the exclusivity of what I offer to earn more?" Let's look at an amazing but actual example of this concept related to serving more people.

Gary Dahl was having drinks with his buddies when the conversation turned to pets. Gary thought that dogs, cats and birds required too much care and money. He joked that he had a pet rock and it was his ideal pet. Dahl spent the next 2 weeks writing a Pet Rock Training Manual. Then he went to a builder's supply store and bought a stone that sold for a penny. He packed the stone in a gift box shaped like a pet carrying case accompanied by the instruction book.

The Pet Rock was introduced at a gift show in San Jose, then in New York. Neiman-Marcus ordered 500! Then Gary sent out homemade news releases of himself accompanied by a picture that showed him surrounded by boxes of his Pet Rocks. Newsweek did a half-page story about the nutty notion, and in less than a year, Gary was shipping 10,000 Pet Rocks EVERY DAY. He appeared on "The Tonight Show," TWICE.

A million rocks sold for $3.95 apiece and in just a few months, and Gary, who decided from the beginning to make at least $1 from every rock, had become a millionaire.

Now you know the Dog Theory of Income. Get a new dog walking client (every other day) for a month and you can earn over $43,000 annually. Sell rocks and you can become a millionaire.

If you research what people make, you'll find that there are people who earn 100K a year selling mops, pails and cleaning tools and others that make less with a Ph.D. and a corporate position with a major company.

What's the lesson here?

Your income will always be in direct proportion to the number of people you serve—it's that simple. Don't just think of something you can do to make money. Ask yourself, "Is what I want to do in demand by enough people who will support me to earn the income I need"?

13

Are You Relevant?

FedEx made their name delivering documents overnight, anywhere in the world. Now that most documents have gone digital, the company had to reinvent itself by changing its technology to stay relevant. It added services to help customers print documents anywhere in the world and to print more easily from mobile devices. Overseas, it added trikes to their truck inventory to access hard to reach places that were not digitally connected.

Their technology now offers customers the option to transmit documents to a copy machine through a USB thumb drive or wirelessly using a smart phone. Customers can also pay for print-outs at the machine and their Print Online service lets people print documents from Google Docs' online cloud storage so they can use the service anywhere they can connect to the Internet.

Their secret to remaining competitive—being relevant. Think about it. A company's interest in hiring you or getting new customers for your business primarily depends on your relevance. Qualifications and experience are important, but relevancy is really the key to getting a call for an interview or an order for your business.

In today's difficult economy, most companies are focused on how they can sustain themselves so that they can be around when the market gets better. Strip away the day-to-day functions of most jobs and you'll find that really only 2 things matter to most employers.

1. **Revenue Relevance**—Maintaining or increasing existing revenue.
2. **Cost Relevance**—Reducing costs.

Think back just a few years ago. The Blackberry was the hot phone to have. Now its market share is dropping fast. The Blackberry brand has lost touch with the current mobile ecosystem. RIM's market share is down by over 50%. Its stock declined from a peak of $70 to less than $24 in 2011. The challenge for Blackberry, Twitter, Facebook or any company is keeping relevant.

By making yourself relevant to a potential employer's revenue or costs you not only differentiate yourself from your competition, but more importantly, you increase the odds of getting an interview because you are in demand with something relevant to offer. What makes you relevant to helping a company make money, save money or solve a problem? You have to be able to answer this question regardless of whether or not you work for a company or you are self-employed.

In the past companies had brand names and few people were a recognized brand. For the most part, unless you were a celebrity, it was unlikely that you could connect with enough people on your own to become a brand recognized by large groups of people. Thanks to the Internet, your age, your education or a big advertising budget are no longer factors in achieving remarkable results.

14

A Lesson in Personal Branding

The Top 4 U.S. brands listed by PSFK.com in 2011 were (1) Google, (2) Apple, (3) Jamie Oliver and (4) MIT.

Look closely at this list. Note # 3 is a person, NOT a company!

Jamie Oliver is an English chef, restaurateur and media personality well known for his growing list of food-focused television shows, his more recent roles in campaigning against the use of processed foods in national schools, and his campaign to change unhealthy diets and poor cooking habits.

Oliver's holding company, Sweet as Candy, has made enough profit for Jamie to have been listed on The Sunday Times list of richest Britons under 30. Oliver's programs are shown in over 40 countries.

Take a look at Justin Bieber, a teen age Canadian singer who started his career at age 12. His performances on YouTube were seen by Scooter Braun, who later became his manager. Braun arranged for him to meet with Usher. Bieber was soon signed to a joint venture between Braun and Usher and then with L.A. Reid and Island Def Jam. His debut single, "One Time" was released worldwide during 2009, and charted within the top 30 in over 10 countries. It was followed by his debut release, My World in November of 2009, which was certified platinum in the US.

Bieber was the first artist to have 7 songs from a debut album chart on Billboard's Hot 100 chart, making him the youngest solo male act to top the chart since Stevie Wonder in 1963. If a teen ager can do this, perhaps YOU can use the power of personal branding to reach your professional goals. Think about it. Bieber essentially started branding himself by uploading a video of him playing the piano on You Tube.

Another great example is Jim Carrey. As a child he performed constantly for anyone who would watch. When he was a teenager, his family was forced to relocate to a Toronto suburb. They all took security and janitorial jobs. Jim worked an 8-hour shift after school. The family lived out of a Volkswagen camper van. Eventually he dropped out of high school (age 16) and decided to strike out into the comedy club scene.

Then he moved to Los Angeles and worked his way into a regular show at The Comedy Store, where he impressed the late Rodney Dangerfield so much that the veteran comic signed him as an opening act for an entire season. After seeing Jim perform, Damon Wayans made a call to his brother, Keenen Ivory Wayans, who was in the process of putting together the sketch comedy show "In Living Color" (1990). Carrey joined the cast and quickly made a name for himself with outrageous acts. Carrey's transformation from TV goofball to marquee headliner happened within 12 MONTHS!

He starred in Ace Ventura: Pet Detective, The Mask and then in Dumb & Dumber, his first multi-million dollar payday! Eventually he made $20 million for a movie (The Cable Guy), the largest up-front sum that had been offered to any comic actor at that time.

Jim wrote himself a check for $10 million dollars in 1983, post-dated 10 years and hoped he could cash it by then. What can we learn from Jim's journey to become a major movie star and comic actor?

- **You Never Get Anything Good For Nothing**—Study the "greats" and you'll see that they all worked hard. It's your focused day-to-day efforts that add up to making you remarkable in what you do.
- **You've got to LOVE what you do**—Studies indicate that 75% of people are not excited about their work—they have a job but they don't have a career—without passion you are unlikely to ever make it big!

- **You've Got To Be Bad Before You Become Great**—Career development is a PROCESS not an event. Keep trying to get better at what you do and sooner or later, you will be the expert!
- **Recognize The Power of Relationships**—Jim made it big because he offered amazing talent that was recognized by industry leaders. Who's in your contact database or who can you add to your contacts that can help you achieve greatness?
- **Focus On Who You Want To Become**—Jim's teenage life started with him working 8 hours after school and living in a Volkswagen van with his family. He beat the odds to become successful because he focused on where he wanted to BE not what he WAS.
- **You Become What You Think About (most often)** Have a focused drive to become somebody great and a WRITTEN plan to make it happen—written goals dramatically increase the chance you will reach them.

Now more than ever, take time to think about what you want out of your life and your career. The Internet and technology have made it easier than ever to become someone great. Look at successful brands and see what you can learn from them to develop your own personal brand. You may never become a celebrity, but you will increase your chances of going from invisible to REMARKABLE!

The power of social media allows you reach a large client or employer base without the large infrastructure required by most businesses in the past. Now there are no age, income or education requirements, just the drive to develop an online presence and the desire to offer something that is remarkable and in demand. The key to the reinvention of who you are is to become someone who can deliver a product or a service that matters. Your goal is to create outcomes that people seek out.

Be passionate about the work you choose. By focusing on work that matters, another amazing thing will occur. You will realize that there's no limit to how much money you can earn. The more people you help to get what they want, the more you will get what you want.

15

What are you earning?
The concept of scarcity

A heart surgeon took his car to his local garage for a regular service, where he usually exchanged a little friendly conversation with the owner. "So tell me," says the mechanic, "I've been wondering about what we both do for a living and how much more you get paid than me." "Look at this he said as he worked on a complicated engine. "I check how it's running, open it up, fix the valves, and put it all back together so it works good as new. We basically do the same job don't we? And yet you are paid 10 times what I am, "How do you explain that?" The surgeon thought for a moment, and smiling replied, "Try it with the engine running."

Your income, more often than not, is related to how easily you can be replaced, or in a sense, related to the scarcity of what you do—translated—how unique is your talent? In today's talent focused market, you need to have clearly defined talent that's tied to something that is scarce and not available as a commodity. Without a defined talent, finding work AND making a great income are almost impossible. Your objective is to provide an incredible value to a very specific and targeted market. Then you need to offer a uniqueness that no one else can match so they'll be compelled to come back for more and they can't help but tell others about their experience with you.

Consider Jonathan Drew who plays "hard to get" with his Acid cigar brand. His stogies are produced in Nicaragua, flavored with wine, oil and herbs and packed in boxes with graffiti-like labels and sold in only 500 stores across the country and on a web site. "The day I go mass market, I'm out of business," says Drew. "When people are in a store they'll buy a

$150 box because they don't know if they will see one again for another three months." Drew sold $1.7 million dollars of Acid cigars in one year.

So how about you? What are you doing with your life, your career, your experience, your abilities and your potential? Are you earning the compensation that offers you the lifestyle you want? Think of a way to become scarce. Then let a targeted group of people know that what you have to offer is unique and valuable. Let's take a look at why income generation is a constantly changing process that requires reinventing yourself over time.

16

American Idol—Insights for YOUR Career

Wouldn't it be nice if you could earn as much as Simon Cowell from American Idol. In 2011 he earned an estimated $21,354 an hour! In his book, *I Don't Mean to Be Rude, But . . .* , he makes a key point about "making it big". Talent isn't enough to get you to the top". He points out that there are a lot of talented people, but getting to the "big time" takes smarts, guts and strategy and in today's business world, that means almost constantly reinventing yourself. He failed boarding school, never went to college and quit job after job when he got bored with them. Then after going through a bankruptcy and having to move in with his parents, he reinvented himself to become the success that he is today.

Jennifer Lopez is another example of how reinventing yourself can be as simple as just trying new things. The latest reinvention for this actress, dancer, singer, and clothes designer is as a judge for American Idol with a $12 million dollar contract. Jennifer has built a $100 million dollar business empire and she is still reinventing herself.

Take a look at Steven Tyler, another American Idol judge. He was the lead singer of Aerosmith—it was his international brand. He was ranked 3rd on Hit Parade's Top 100 Metal Vocalists of All Time. In 2001 he was inducted into the Rock and Roll Hall of Fame. Now he's 63, almost retired, yet through constant reinvention, he is making $12 million a year on American Idol.

Research successful people in business today and you will see an interesting common denominator. Most of them have built highly valued skills that are IN DEMAND and they are constantly reinventing themselves. What can we learn from Cowell, Lopez and Tyler about reinvention as it relates to our own careers?

- Your ultimate career success might be 3 or 4 jobs away—plan for where you want to be in 2 years.
- Decide what you want and build a bridge to get where you want to be.
- Think about how you can help others FIRST and then watch how they will help you with your career—give to get.
- Don't rest on your success or you could end up being a "one-hit wonder".
- You can't count on one particular accomplishment or job skill—EXPECT to reinvent yourself.
- Re-craft your skills for new opportunities that give you OPTIONS.
- Once you accept that you're probably going to have multiple careers, your vision should change from "What are my qualifications?" to "What does it take to get to where I want to be?"
- Realize that after 2 years doing most jobs, your learning and development curve is flat.
- Forget about stability—think marketability!
- Decide today what is it that you would really like to be.

In an era where there are so many new ways to do everything, the middle of the road is the road to nowhere. Reinvent yourself to become marketable (remarkable) and in demand. To truly be remarkable, you must commit to becoming exceptional in whatever you intend to offer as a product or service to an employer or a customer. Let's take a look at the music business to understand the difference between good versus great.

17

Brown M&M's—A Lesson for Success

Van Halen is an American band that sold 80 million albums worldwide and during the 80's, they had more Billboard Hot 100 hits than any other rock band. They are the 19th best-selling band of all time with sales of over 56 million albums in the US. On stage, the musicians looked like a wild bunch of crazy guys who seemed carefree and just showed up to have fun playing music.

But if you knew what happened before they came on stage, you might have thought about these guys in a different way. They did dozens of shows every year, and at each venue, their band would show up with 9 semi trucks full of gear. Because of the technical requirements to produce a show, the band's contract was very complex. A typical contract might include a clause that read, "There will be 15 power sockets at 20-foot spaces providing 19 amperes." But one clause in its touring contract demanded a bowl of M&Ms be backstage with all the brown M&Ms removed. Van Halen hid a special clause in the middle of the contract. It read, "There will be no brown M&Ms in the backstage area, and if there are any, it is grounds to cancel the show with full compensation. When David Roth would arrive at a new venue, he'd walk backstage and glance at the M&M bowl. If he saw a brown M&M, he'd demand a line check of the entire production. It was his way of seeing if the technicians had read the contract. He was an operations expert, not a technician. He couldn't spend hours every night checking the amperage of each socket. He needed a way to assess quickly whether the stage hands at each venue were paying attention.

More often than not, success in your job search, an interview and success in your life comes from paying attention to the details. Artists sometimes make it look too easy.

Michael Jackson once said, "Nobody could duplicate Fred Astaire's ability to dance, but what I never stop trying to emulate is his total discipline, his absolute dedication to every aspect of his art. He rehearsed, rehearsed, and rehearsed until he got it just the way he wanted it. It was Fred Astaire's work ethic that few people ever discussed and even fewer could ever hope to equal." It's the attention to details that make you a professional or an amateur.

What's the brown M&M in your life? Notice the words, "your life".

Too many people use the term THE world failing to see that in reality, the only thing you can truly control is YOUR world. That's why tracking the results you get from your efforts can help you keep focused on what matters in your life, instead of watching television and vicariously living your life by watching the adventures of others.

18

What's Happening in YOUR World?

The news reports say car sales are up and the global economy is expected to improve by 10%. But you know, those statistics really have no impact on you. The year ahead will only be better if YOU make it better. Stop worrying about global and national events, and start taking action focused on YOUR situation. It's not about the national employment market, it's about YOUR market and YOUR career. Stop spending 90% of your time watching the news, and concentrate 90% on how the news affects YOU.

What's happening in business is far more important than who got shot, what the movie of the year is, or what celebrity made $50 million selling clothes. You need to have balance in your life but too many people focus on others success and do little to achieve anything in their life. I love the phrase, "How is that working for you?" If what you've been doing isn't helping you make the money you need or getting you closer to your goals, NOW is the time to change or 12 months from now you will probably be right where you are now. Remember, you can't manage it if you can't measure it. Write down EXACTLY what you want to achieve and then track your progress in reaching your goals. Decide to become one of the 3% of people that have clearly defined and WRITTEN goals. There's something magical about having goals in writing and then looking at them when you wake up and when you go to bed. Start today to change your thoughts to change YOUR world!

It's been said that you are nothing but the sum of your current thoughts at a given time and you will become what you think about most of the time. Assuming that's true, let's look at how to get started building your own personal brand.

19

It's a Brand New World

Start right now. As of this moment you need to think of yourself differently! Starting today you are a brand. Recognize that we now live in a project based employment marketplace. Almost all work today is organized into tasks called projects. I think we should all forget about the word "resume"." It should be called a marketing brochure or a personal branding profile. Instead of a list of titles and job descriptions, your marketing brochure (resume) should bring to life the skills you've mastered, the projects you've delivered and essentially what makes you remarkable. If you're treating your resume as if it's a marketing brochure, you've learned the 1st concept of being a free agent, the way most people will be working in the years to come.

The 2nd concept is one that most of today's professional athletes have already learned—you've got to check with the market on a regular basis to get feedback on your brand's value. You don't have to be looking for a job to go on a job interview. Don't wait until you need to find a job to evaluate where you stand with your personal brand. Ask for and insist on honest feedback about your performance and regularly assess your market value. You need to know what you are worth on the open market. Forget about what jobs are available and think more in terms of who needs what you have to offer and begin to sell yourself as something of value to a business or person that needs your help.

It's over. There are no more corporate ladders. That's not the way careers work anymore. A career is now a checkerboard that involves moves that go sideways, forward and even go backward when it makes sense. A career is a portfolio of projects that should teach you new skills, offer you new expertise, develop new capabilities and constantly reinvent you as a brand.

If you've been doing the same job for 5-10 years it's probably time for a change. Your ability to periodically reinvent yourself will determine your future survival. Today, major companies are outsourcing many of the tasks associated with building their products. They farm out "projects" to anywhere in the world where they can be completed at the lowest possible cost.

Consider the Apple iPad. No Apple employee has ever assembled an iPad or built the circuit board. If Apple employees built the iPad instead of just designing it, an iPad would probably cost around $4,000.

The best example of personal branding in the world right now is Lady Gaga. We haven't seen a brand expand this fast in years.

She sold over 300 million albums in her 1st year and amassed a net worth of $40 million dollars in 24 months. She was only 24 years old at the time.

Perhaps even more amazing is Jessica Simpson. Her fashion and accessories brand includes shoes, jeans, swimwear, watches and fragrances. She sold almost $1 billion dollars worth of products in 12 months.

Ask yourself these questions:

What turns you on? Are you learning something new? What is your personal definition of success? However you answer these questions, search relentlessly for jobs or projects that lead you to what you want in your life. Don't settle for anything less.

You are a brand. You are in charge of your brand. There is no single path to success. And there is no one right way to create your brand. Only one thing is for sure. Start today. Most people never get started in becoming remarkable because of "fear of failure'. Years of research have identified this phobia as the # 1 killer of great ideas. It's time to think of failure in a new way.

20

Failures Are Investments—Not Losses

So often when we are rejected for a job or don't get selected for an interview, it's easy to feel down and wonder, "What's wrong with me?" Just because you didn't get what you wanted doesn't mean that you've lost something.

Susan Boyle used all her savings to pay for a professionally cut demo, copies of which she later sent to record companies, radio talent competitions and local/national TV stations. After Boyle won several local singing competitions, her mother urged her to enter Britain's Got Talent and take the risk of singing in front of an audience larger than her parish church. Boyle abandoned an audition for The X Factor because she believed people were being chosen for their looks. She almost gave up her plan to enter Britain's Got Talent believing she was too old.

But the following year, Boyle applied for an audition for the 3rd series of Britain's Got Talent and was accepted as a contestant. Amazingly, she was one of 40 acts made it through to the semi-finals. She was favored to win the final but ended up in 2nd place to a competitor. But she didn't give up.

Boyle's first album became Amazon's best-selling album in pre-sales, 3 months before its scheduled release. Susan's debut album was recognized as the fastest selling UK debut album of all time selling 411,820 copies. Her album sold 701,000 copies in the US its first week, the best opening week for a debut artist in over a decade. Boyle gave a U.S. concert tour in November and appeared in her own television special—it was the TV Guide Network's highest rated television special in its history. In May 2010, Susan Boyle was voted by Time magazine as the 7th most influential person in the world, 14 places above Barack Obama, who received one fifth the number of her votes.

Going from good to great takes persistence and failure is a natural and normal part of getting to where you need to be. How bad to you want it? Make failure an investment and use it to get the job and a career that you are excited about! Susan's secret was that she looked forward versus backward to realize her dream of becoming a professional singer. Let's look at how a simple way of thinking can radically transform your career.

21

Zero Based Thinking

"If I weren't working at this job today, knowing what I know now, would I get into it again?" The principle of zero based thinking, popularized by Brian Tracy in his books and seminars is simply making decisions looking forward rather than backward. Start today and call today zero.

Set aside how much time, money and effort you've invested in your career. Then ask this question, "If I do what I've been doing and I get what I've been getting, is it worthwhile to continue in this career track?" It's been said that efficiency is doing things right but effectiveness is doing the right things. Using zero based thinking helps you identify the right things. Ask these questions to get your thinking on track to reinvent yourself:

- What do you really want to do?
- Are you getting what you want out of your career or are you just working hoping something better comes along?
- If you weren't working at this job today, knowing what you know now, would you get into it again?
- If you could change things in an instant, what would you really like to be doing?
- Have you "reality tested" your perceptions about the job market?
- Do you have real facts that support your decision to stay in your job or look for something else?

Zero-based thinking is powerful because it opens up a world of possibilities that we otherwise might not consider. It frees our minds to think without any sense of commitment tied to past decisions or actions. Ask yourself, "What I can do to align my life with what I really want so I can begin to reinvent myself?" Focus on factors that are under your control and actions that you can take to shape your future.

Perhaps the auto industry can offer us some insight into how this works. Let's take a look.

22

Kaizen Your Way to Job Search Success

Companies like Toyota are famous for using a "kaizen approach" in a manufacturing setting to maximize efficiency. Kaizen (Japanese for "improvement" or "change for the better") refers to a philosophy that focuses on continuous improvement—incremental changes that over time can create dramatic results. Although it's most commonly thought of as being related to manufacturing, I think its core principles are ideally matched to success in finding a job. Consider kaizen as the science of small steps that tricks your brain into forgetting the fear of failure and other self-sabotaging tendencies that can derail your efforts. The idea is simple: take small, incremental steps toward your job search goal every day. Focus on small improvements rather than on the final goal of finding a job. Consider these "changes" to maximize the success of your job search strategy:

Look For New Opportunities With Different Thinking.

Albert Einstein said that "Insanity is doing the same thing over and over again but expecting different results"—Are you doing the same thing over and over in your job search and expecting different results?

Switch Your Thinking from BEING qualified to becoming competitively marketable.

If you aren't getting results with what you have, what steps do you need to take to improve what you can offer?

Stand Out!

What can you do to enhance your chances of being recognized and winning a job offer? Lady Gaga earned a net worth of $40 million in just 2 years because she figured out a way to stand out.

Stop Looking For Opportunities That Don't Exist.

Many job searchers tend to look for jobs they have recently done and they just keep looking hoping they will find something that matches their current role. If you aren't getting results, don't keep investing your time and effort where there doesn't appear to be a demand for what you are offering. Figure out what you can offer as transferable talent that could be a great match for a new line of work where there are openings. By integrating kaizen into your job search planning, you may discover that reinventing yourself a little each day should be your goal to achieve economic stability. Despite what you might think, economic security does NOT lie in your job; it lies in your own power to offer something of value.

23

Solve Problems by Copying Success

When we analyze a complicated problem like a married couple considering a divorce, or a business approaching a bankruptcy, we often try to come up with a solution that matches the scale of the problem. If the problem is a round hole with a 30 inch diameter, our brains will go looking for a 30 inch peg to fill it.

If a child brings home a report card with five A's and an F, it makes sense to focus on the F. But what if you switched your focus from the problem with the F and concentrated on what your child did to get the A's.

Consider looking for the "hidden diamonds" by asking what things are working or have worked in the past that are working for you and see if there is a pattern that can help you discover a solution to the problem. Focusing on these "hidden diamonds" can be counter intuitive for businesses and people faced with an unexpected change in their career track, yet this approach may be exactly what you need to find a breakthrough solution.

Perhaps the Ford Motor Company turn-around and the story of a pharmaceutical firm can offer us some insights.

Alan Mulally was CEO material who got the top job at Ford after identifying just 2 key improvement areas for the company. Mulally is proof that a single, extraordinary leader with vision focused on what works can make all the difference in an organization.

In 2006, Bill Ford, Jr., went shopping for someone to take over the CEO role and he found his man, the father of the Boeing 777 airliner at Boeing, an aircraft manufacturer. Industry observers were shocked because never had someone without any automotive experience ever been the CEO of the company. Before he took the job, Mulally spent a lot of time with Bill Ford and the senior management team to learn as much as he could about the culture of the firm and its competitive position and he focused on what had made Ford successful in the past, rather than what was wrong with the company.

Mulally's plan was to focus the company on its core brand and get rid of other brands they owned (Jaguar and Volvo) and get a $23 billion line of credit to help restructure the company. That credit line enabled Ford to invest in product development of what had been successful and revived their product line with improved vehicles that had been their major money makers. As a result, Ford was the only firm of the Big 3 auto makers that did not have to take any government bailout money. Now Ford is on the road to recovery, focused on their core expertise and free from most of the problems that made it non-competitive in the past.

Another example of how focusing on success instead of a problem to get results, comes from the pharmaceutical industry involving a new product release. A company launched a drug which had been viewed as a miracle drug for minimizing asthma attacks, yet several months after launch, the company's sales remained way below expectations. A team was organized to help figure out why the drug was underperforming. They immediately started looking for "hidden diamonds" and soon they found some.

Two salesmen were selling 25 times more of the drug than their peers. Rather than selling the health benefits of the drug, the salesman helped doctors understand how to administer it. The drug required infusion via an intravenous drip which was unfamiliar to the doctors who would be prescribing the drug. By changing their focus on what was working, sales increased dramatically.

If you are looking to find a job, figure out a way to reinvent yourself capitalizing on your strengths and relating your talent to what's in demand (focus on employer needs). Sell yourself based on what makes you valuable instead of just telling employers what you have done.

24

Get Exactly What You Want—
Not What's Available

So many times you may have heard, "you become what you think about most often". Hidden within that statement is a key component that many of us forget. It all comes down to your personal expectation as to whether or not you're going to ultimately succeed.

That's where it all starts. You're not going to get anything if you don't work hard to achieve it. But you're not going to work hard in the first place unless you have a strong enough expectation that you'll be successful. This is how life works. Your motivation to take action, and to follow through until the job is done, is directly proportional to your belief that you will succeed.

When you believe that success is going to be the end result of you never giving up, then you are going to attack your objective with a greater passion. You're going to be excited about what you're doing, because you know that it matters. You know that whatever it is you're doing, it will eventually translate into the result you want. When you believe strongly enough that you will succeed at something, success is practically guaranteed—not because your belief creates the result, but because you don't give up taking dedicated action until you get what you want. The perspective of certainty is what gives you the ability to see obstacles as challenges that fuel your growth. Focus on "How can I, instead of why can't I?"

The late author Dorothea Brande, in her book, *Wake Up and Live*, wrote, "Live as though it was impossible to fail." You'll know when what you decide to do is the right thing. Just don't get "analysis paralysis" and never get started. If you've got a major goal you want to achieve, here are 3 things to keep in mind:

- **You need to have the expectation that you (specifically YOU) can achieve this goal.**

  People typically have a lot easier time believing something is "possible" than believing it's possible for them." They don't fully believe that they will be capable of achieving a goal because they are missing something—the time, the talent or the resources.

- **You have to have the expectation that you will close the resource gap, no matter how wide it is.**

  How can you compete with a dyslexic college kid like Richard Branson, who took on the music industry and the airlines (and succeeded)? A lack of time, money, connection, it doesn't matter, because there's a number of creative solutions out there that you're going to come up with to overcome them. If you have the expectation that it will eventually be resolved, guess what's going to happen?

- **You have to have the expectation that every action you take matters.**

  Recognize that action accumulates. The pyramids were built brick by brick.

Once you have your goals clearly defined, it's time to think about how you can "date" an employer or a new customer.

25

Create Content to Generate New Customers (Employers)

Creating content can supercharge your ability to get new customers (potential employers). Think of what your success rate would be if you asked every first date if they loved you. You wouldn't think of doing that would you? So why try to get business by asking for "the sale" before you develop a relationship? A strong content strategy can bring emotion and context to your personal brand and attract employers or customers to your business. Consider this model for personal branding to get employers (customers) to notice you.

Educate—Publicize—Convert

Educate—Tell Before You Sell

Bring potential customers (employers) to you with great content that they are interested in and will seek out. Content connects people to you, and it's more effective when it's viral. Content can be advice as to how to solve a problem, a way to make or save more money or expertise on how to develop a product.

Publicize

Share your content via blogs, twitter and videos. If nobody notices your content, it's worthless. Leverage your content to help you manage the syndication of your content across the Web. When valuable content appears on a site where prospects (employers) are already in the mindset of looking for what you have to offer, it's an easy transition for them to click-through to your website and learn more. Fans are more likely to share great content than telling their friends about advertising they've seen.

Convert

Consider the blog "The Fence Post" hosted by a fencing company. By simply starting a blog offering tips on how to use fencing products, the company generated an 800% increase in leads. By educating potential customers about ways to use fencing to improve their landscaping, decorate their yard and protect their plants, the company started a blog that evolved into a community forum to discuss a variety of landscape topics and built a reader base that dramatically expanded their business. Using these concepts, let's examine the difference between selling versus telling.

26

Are You Searching or Selling?

Many things have changed in the world of work and job search in the past 12 months. Tried and true methods still apply, but the impact of the Internet and a recovering job market require building a different kind of job search strategy that is much more proactive and focuses more on "selling" than just "telling".

Some new rules and some old rules.

Be Flexible In Thinking about Your Concept of a "Job".

Don't assume that your next job will be a full-time position with one company. Temp to perm and portfolio careers (a mix of part-time employment, temporary jobs, freelancing, interim consulting, self-employment), have become viable strategies. Creating INCOME security, instead of JOB security is the new way of thinking.

Be Clear On What Job You Seek and Target Companies Where You Can Add Value.

Frame your job search strategy around target employers so that everything you put on the Internet will resonate with them. Realize that in your job search, you're in the middle of a sales and marketing campaign for your company (i.e., YOU) in which you're selling your value proposition. Research your target companies to position yourself as an informed and engaged candidate in interviews.

Compile a list of at 10 companies that match your career needs and identify the key decision makers within each one.

Google the decision makers' names to find out where they hang out online and how you can connect with them. Here's your chance to circumvent the gatekeepers by identifying and connecting directly with top decision makers and tap into the hidden job market of unadvertised positions.

Learn about the culture of each company and determine what their needs are so you can develop your value proposition around their needs. Set up Google Alerts to give you up-to-the-minute news on your target employers and their decision makers.

Define Your "Personal Brand" and Amplify It In Your Personal Marketing Communications.

Personal branding is all about defining the unique set of strengths, personal attributes and passions that differentiate you from your peers. Branding makes it easier for hiring decision makers to determine whether you're a good fit for their organization.

The Job Search Landscape Has Changed—So Has The Resume.

Remember that the resume is a marketing document, not a just a career history. Include just enough information to capture attention and compel people to contact you. Precision writing with an underlying branding strategy are key. Everything in your resume should align with your target employers' needs. With more people looking for work, your sales package (the resume) has to be remarkable or you will never get noticed.

Create A Searchable Linked-in Profile.

Enhance your profile's search ability by using embedded key words and integrate a powerful branding theme into your professional profile.

Build A Strong e-Brand.

Surveys show that the majority of recruiters and hiring managers search online when they're sourcing and assessing top talent. Design a personal marketing strategy to consistently communicate your unique talents across multiple channels, online and offline.

Get Published Using a Blog To Showcase Your Subject Matter Expertise.

Consider using eblogger from Google. It's free and you can be up and running in less than an hour. Build up keyword-rich content so you're more likely to be found when people search topics related to your specialization.

Use The Strategic Positioning Value Of Twitter.

On Twitter you can take advantage of the cross-branding power of LinkedIn's Twitter application, which display your most recent tweets. With no extra effort, a simple tweet is displayed on your linked-in profile and is searchable by millions of people globally.

27

If You Do What You've Been Doing

If your job search seems to be going nowhere, it may be time to change your approach. Too many job searchers keep doing the same thing without getting any results. If the fish aren't biting, it's time to change the bait. If they still aren't biting, then it may be time to try another lake. Consider these options:

Add Testimonials

Watch TV infomercials and you'll find that at least 30-50% of the program is made up of testimonials from happy customers. That's no accident. Testimonials can be incredibly powerful in your resume. Consider adding brief quotes from clients or managers.

Utilize the Power of Advanced Social Networking

Take your job search to Twitter or other social networking sites, so you can maximize your exposure. Become a fan of an employer's Facebook page and get engaged. Explore networking sites to discover internal networking tools to help you link with people that can hire you or refer you to someone that may have a position opening.

Instead Of Just Focusing on Your Strengths, Strengthen Your Weaknesses

While you should focus on what things you do well, consider that those aren't the things that need work. If you know you look good on paper and you get a lot of interviews, but nothing happens after that, perhaps you need to focus on improving your interviewing skills. Consider the story of Remy Piazza, from Toronto.

Remy made a list of 50 employers, researched them, narrowed his list to 20, and then he picked 5 that he really wanted to work for. Piazza focused his time and effort on appealing to those 5 decision makers who could hire him. Then he sent an email chain letter to people in his network, asking for help. In his email, Piazza listed his target employers and asked readers for an introduction to anyone they knew who worked there, sold to them, or bought from them. (It's not just people who work at an employer who can help, but also that employer's vendors and clients.) Finally, he asked recipients to forward the email to 10 other people. If 10 people forward it to 10 people, an email can reach 10,000 readers in just 3 cycles. He got a lot of new contacts doing this, including meetings with CEO's, VP's, and other executives. Then learned all he could about them, tapping Linked-in and other resources for information. He spent an average of 8 hours of research on each employer.

Armed with a list of facts regarding an employer's problems, needs, and possible solutions, Piazza started calling on top executives to ask for a meeting. His calls were focused on the employer's needs. He understood what they were going through and told them how he could add value. One of the 5 target employers offered him a job.

If you do what you've been doing, you'll get what you've been getting. What can you do different to change your job search results?

28

Things Most People Don't Know About Finding a Job

Job seekers today are facing a never before seen employment marketplace with new rules and new technologies. Gone are the days were you could just post your resume on-line and wait for a call. Consider adding these components to your job search.

1. **Share Stories Not Facts**

   There's an old adage in sales and marketing that stories sell and facts tell. People can relate personally to stories. Be able to tell a story of how you helped a company make money, save money or solve a problem. Don't just quote statistics or speak of your skills in general terms.

2. **Present Solutions**

   An employer wants to hire someone to solve a particular problem. Either they don't have enough of something or they want to change something. If they had all the solutions then they wouldn't need you. After you have thoroughly researched and analyzed the company, its culture, the competition, the industry and the people you are interviewing with, you need to know what potential solutions they may need and be able to communicate your ability to solve them. Any employer worth working for will be completely impressed not only by your research but by your effort.

3. **Be Proactive**

Most people don't want to put in the time and effort to do what they need to do to secure an interview and a job. The vast majority of jobs are attained by active networking—not by posting your resume on-line or applying for job after job. Yet most people are not willing to do what it takes to establish and nurture the right networks. Focusing on building relationships can mean the difference between having or not having network contacts and ultimately getting a job.

4. **Be Interesting**

Surveys of recruiters and HR managers show that the #1 trait that job seekers lack is high energy. People want to be around other people who are upbeat, exciting and at the very least, energetic. If you're not excited about what you have to offer, why should anyone else?

5. **Speak Multiple Languages**

People get information in 3 ways; auditory, kinesthetic and visual. Auditory learners can grasp information just by you talking to them. Visual learners need some form of pictures or stories to create the picture before they "get it". Kinesthetic learners need to be an active participant before the information gets through to them. Most people are visual. Try to appeal to an interviewer's preferred style. It's difficult to be sure what the interviewer prefers, so make an effort communicate in all 3 styles. Why do you think that Google paid big dollars for YouTube? Because video appeals to the masses in a way that written text never could. A video on your personal website can produce amazing results.

6. **Don't Be A Quitter**

Most people quit too soon. Studies show that 81% of professional sales people take 5 calls to close a sale. However, 90% give up prior to making that critical 5th call—48% quit after the first call and another 24% quit after the second call.

7. **Have A Remarkable Resume**

Your resume might get you an interview but it can also lose it for you. Make an investment in a resume prepared by a professional. You need to work with someone who knows what employers want and can make your resume sell, not just tell. The # 1 reason someone initially reviews your resume is to rule you OUT!

8. **Be a Giver Not a Taker**

If you are always looking for what a company is going to do for you and what your benefits will be, then you are thinking backwards. Everyone's favorite radio station is WIIFM (what's in it for me). Focus on what you can do to help the employer as a solution provider instead of a job searcher.

It's a buyer's market so you better have the right product. Now more than ever, make your job search a process, not just an event. 90% of job searchers post their resume on-line and wait for a call. 10% of job searchers build relationships. Most jobs are filled through referrals and relationships with people. Focus on people, not postings, and the results may surprise you.

29

You are What You Believe

A major role of our unconscious mind is to filter the millions of bits of information that we're bombarded with every day and we delete and generalize them, so we can focus on what we think is important. When we change our focus, the world around us presents us with evidence that supports our new thoughts. Our brain likes making sense of the world, so despite the many contradictions you may encounter, you will find supporting details for your beliefs. In the book, "The Secret", it says, "Whatever you focus on will expand and be brought to your conscious awareness".

Think about your biggest challenge in life right now. If you spend your time thinking about a problem, your unconscious brain will filter all the information being thrown at you and present you with more evidence to support the problem. Your brain likes being right. TRY SHIFTING YOUR FOCUS FROM THE PROBLEM TO THE SOLUTION.

What is it you really want to accomplish? The problem shouldn't be your focus. Professional athletes focus on the ideal outcome and then visualize all the steps necessary to make it happen.

Focus on the ideal solution long enough, and your brain will shift gears. It will start providing evidence (evidence that is already around you, but not consciously recognized) that you can use to work towards the solution and around or through the problem.

30

Music and Jobs—A Clue for Success

When you watch the Grammy Awards, it appears that the recording industry is going strong. But at the end of 2009, the music business was worth 50% of what it was 10 years ago and the decline doesn't look like it's going to slow down.

Revenue from U.S. music sales and licensing dropped to $6.3 billion in 2009. 1999 revenues were $14.6 billion. There have been a lot of changes over the past 10 years as to how, when and where we listen to music.

In 1999, Napster, a free online file-sharing service, made its debut. Not only did Napster help change the way most people got music, it also lowered the price point from $14 for a CD to free. Even after iTunes got people buying music tracks for just 99 cents, it wasn't as attractive as free.

When Plushgun released its album "Pins and Panzers," it was the most downloaded album on a popular peer-to-peer Website with 100,000 illegal downloads. Unauthorized downloads continue to represent about 90% of the market. The problems for the music industry may offer us a clue as to how we need to focus our job search strategy. Despite declining music sales, the Internet has exposed consumers to more music than ever before.

Free downloads are a problem for the music industry primarily due to a supply and demand problem where customers can get what they want for free. Yet an artist can often sell more music because of the greater exposure. Once people know you, they may buy from you, but first they need to know about what you have to offer. Exposure is the key.

Think of how you can leverage digital networks to get in front of more people by being "free". Hiring employees is costly when you factor in advertising and recruiting costs. You essentially become "free" if you find THEM and self yourself directly with a digital identity. Essentially YOU become the free peer-to-peer network connection.

31

Pocket Agents—
The New Digital Workforce

Mobile apps continue to evolve as digital butlers to help us with many tasks formerly handled by customer service representatives. Look closely and you'll see that most applications have a built in branding component. The marketing strategy integrated into each application is to make consumers' lives easier when they need it most, remind them of your company name and hope that they're more likely to become loyal customers.

Branded phone apps are taking the place of labor intensive customer service and they're always available in your pocket.

Consider this smart phone application.

State Farm lets customers look up policy information, record accident details and submit claims on their phone. It's a free application with features for all consumers, whether or not they're already customers. Its On the Road feature, uses the iPhone's GPS to help users find the nearest hotel or gas station or call a tow truck, taxi, locksmith or rental car service. A built-in checklist reminds drivers what to do when they're in an accident and included is a way to look for nearby agents, including State Farm Agents. Existing customers can do all that plus look up their policy information, record accident details and submit claims, including photos of the accident taken with their smart phone cameras.

Serving as a sort of mobile brand builder, these Pocket Agents are just one of many examples of the myriad new opportunities enabled by the iPhone and Android platforms. As you look for work or consider changing jobs, study the changing world of work and figure out how your talents can complement new technologies. Your employability depends on your awareness of these changes and your creativity in reinventing yourself to add value to these new business models.

32

Failure as a Formula for Success

So often people feel like great opportunities have passed them by or they've lost a job and see no hope for their future. The secret to recovery is more often than not, reframing your mindset to think of failure as a formula for success. The more you try, the better your odds of success. Consider these guys who made this formula work.

> Jim Dyson is an engineer who made a fortune designing vacuum cleaners. He spent 6 years developing a different kind of vacuum cleaner trying over 5,000 prototypes. Each year he got more into debt eventually owing $4 million to his creditors. He had 3 mortgages on his house. Everybody thought he was crazy. He repaid his bank loan within 4 months of selling his first product. Today his estimated net worth is $1.6 billion.

> 6 years before they came up with idea for Guitar Hero, Kai and Charles Huang ran a company that almost filed for bankruptcy 3 times. They borrowed $500,000 from a family friend and were $2 million in debt when they launched the original video game. Guitar Hero II sold $200 million in 2006. In 2007, Guitar Hero III generated sales of $1 billion. The video game publisher Activision later bought RedOctane for $100 million.

In today's employment market, it's the persistent and open-minded person who can come up with a solution for a new career or a recreate themselves with a new way to package their talents that will be a success. Use the tools of technology to distribute your talents, keeping in mind that your income will always be in direct proportion to the number of people you serve.

33

Think Like a Competitor

Your qualifications are a key factor in you getting hired however the impact of competition is a variable that many job searchers forget. There are an average of 1 million job listings and over 40 million resumes posted on Monster.com. CareerBuilder distributes its resumes to over 1000 local newspapers and job search websites.

With an average of 40 million people on job boards looking for work, how will you be noticed?

If you are an IT professional, you are competing with millions of workers worldwide in today's plug and play web linked services market. Consider the impact of logmein.com. It allows anyone in the world to access a Mac or PC from any Web browser in real time. If you are a Network Engineer in Thailand, you can essentially compete with anyone in the U.S.

A company advertises for a sales account manager and gets 2000 resumes. 10 applicants have a personal website link embedded on their resume highlighting what they can offer along with a blog link that offers insights into how to develop sales strategies. 5 show up on Linked-in and 7 were referred by current employees who met the candidates at a sales conference. Who gets an interview?

Understanding how to compete with your competition and creativity thinking about ways to get noticed is what can make the difference in getting hired or getting ignored. Build a digital profile of who you are and what you have to offer. Then give someone a reason to pick you.

34

Are You Fishing With The Right Bait?

Great jobs posted on-line can generate 3000+ responses in a day. Hard to believe isn't it? When the Apple store (24/7) opened in New York City, there were 300 openings and 10,000 people applied!

Standing out in a competitive employment market can be difficult. Now more than ever, the resume can make or break your job search. Unlike a few years ago when people brought their resume direct to a company or requested a meeting with a Hiring Manager, today's job search protocol is essentially 100% digitally based.

Although some small companies welcome an unsolicited face-to-face meeting with a potential employee, you should focus your attention on using an electronic resume. Consider these points to get an interview.

- **Companies Prefer A Digital Copy Of Your Resume.** It can be easily stored, sent to hiring managers via email and tracked by an Applicant Tracking Systems (ATS). If you apply to a large company, expect them to use an ATS that relies on key words. Consider adding key words that do not appear in the body of your resume in a small font at the bottom of your resume. These words, separated by a semi-colon (;) act like a bar code or computer meta-tag that links your resume to keyword searches commonly used by recruiters and employers. Use words that include cities/states/zip codes where you might want to work, local area codes, part-time, full time, bi-lingual etc. Think of what a recruiter or employer might use in a key word search to find you. For example: Keywords: 305;954;561;San Diego; Spanish; relocate;

commission only; Macintosh; Lion ;security clearance; supervisor; international travel; CPA; ESOL; ISO9000; southeast; MCSE

- **Electronic Resumes Can Link an Employer Directly to Your Personal Website** using an embedded URL (www.yourname. com) right from your resume. From there a Hiring Manager can access your LinkedIn profile, your blog, Twitter account and even videos you can add to LinkedIn or embed on your website.

- **Help Employers & Recruiters Find Your Resume on Google.** A great way you can display yourself in a professional manner and increase the chances of being seen by recruiters and employers, is to publish your resume online through Google Docs. This will also allow you access to a web version of your resume at any time, making sharing simple. Most importantly, your resume can be indexed by Google, so that a search of your name will get your resume in front of the right people.

To make it easier for recruiters and hiring managers to find you on-line, Google has a step-by-step guide on how to host your resume online using Google Docs. After your resume is hosted with Google Docs, it's time to share it. It's simple. Here's how to do it.

1. Sign up for an account with a URL shortener. Consider using bitly.com, however there are many other URL shorteners with built-in tracking and analytics.
2. After you are signed in, copy and paste the URL of your hosted resume in Google Docs into the large link field. Then click the Customize button.
3. Enter your personalized bit.ly link in the customize field that appears and click "Shorten." That's it! Consider creating personalized links to other pages that you refer people to during your job search as well, such as cover letters, your LinkedIn profile, Twitter account, blog or webpage.

Now when a potential employer looks you up online, they can find your resume easily and by creating a customized link to your resume with Bit.ly, you can track when someone clicks to view your resume.

- **Define Your Accomplishments At Past Positions**. You need accomplishment stories for your resume. Did you create a new tracking system that helped the company become more efficient? Did you save a significant amount of money by eliminating unnecessary expenses? Think back to your achievements and provide numbers whenever possible to quantify your accomplishments. Not only are stories more impressive, they are a great lead-in to your accomplishments during an interview.

If you were reading resumes and you saw the following lines on two different resumes, which one would get your attention?

A. Created an incentive program to reduce absenteeism.
B. Created an incentive program reducing absenteeism by 20% in less than 3 months.

Do you see the difference? The second statement is definable (quantified), easy to understand, and relates a skill tied to measurable results.

- **Identify an Employer's Pain Points.** Most people buy benefits not features. It's not the fact that a car has a button which switches it from 2-wheel drive into 4-wheel drive that they're interested in, but the fact that when they press that button they can drive through mud without getting stuck.

For job seekers, selling benefits rather than features is important. One of the key ways that you can do that is by identifying a prospective employer's pain points and then demonstrating how you can help to solve them.

Where can you look to find out what issues and problems a company is facing?

1. **The company's website**—sometimes it's possible to read between the lines by looking at whether the company is diversifying into different areas, is opening new branches or closing existing ones or has recently won new contracts. Changes to hiring patterns or advertisements for key positions in the organization can also provide clues that the company is facing problems that you might be able to help them solve. Check out newspaper articles, articles in trade magazines, press releases and online articles and reports for clues as to what is going on in the inside.
2. **Competitor's activities**—Sometimes moves and changes related to a competitor can provide hints as to the type of pressures that an organization might be experiencing.
3. **Networking contacts**—Stay tuned in to your network for insider information and don't forget that informational interviews can often reveal the types of issues that businesses are facing.

You goal is to find out what a company needs that you can help them with. Try to find out why they are currently hiring for this position. Do your research on the company and show them you've implemented related solutions in the past.

Packaging is Important.

Your resume is your package—make it SELL not just tell! A resume is NOT an application. Most resumes list tasks from job descriptions and essentially tell the reader what you have done in terms of tasks that you performed.

Reposition yourself as TALENT highlighting what you can do to improve revenue or save money. A great way to show cost savings is to highlight how you can improve processes or decrease time to deliver a product. Consider these points:

Your Resume Is a "Marketing Piece" NOT Just A Summary Of What You Have Done.

1. The average resume is read in 10-15 SECONDS by an administrative office person looking for keywords—it's unlikely that hiring managers will see your resume if you get screened out the 1st time.

2. The initial reason someone reads your resume is to rule you OUT!

3. Eliminate words or phrases that are rejection factors. A common rejection phrase is "with 30 years of experience". For most resume screeners, this just means you are getting old!

4. In the first 5 seconds, a reader should know what type of position you are looking for—i.e. Graphics Designer.

5. Optimize your resume by including key words so you can be found by employers and recruiters using Boolean Searches. If you're applying for a position at a larger firm, your resume will likely be among thousands of resumes that corporate recruiters receive.

If You Don't Use the Right Keywords, You'll Probably Never Even Be Seen.

6. Many large companies are using a keyword-searchable database that scans resumes for words related to certain job vacancies. To figure out what keywords are vital to your position, analyze job postings to see what keywords are repeatedly mentioned related to the job title you are pursuing.

   Consider using LinkedIn's skills section to find the keywords that would most likely be used in a company's search query database. Click on the "More" tab in your LinkedIn profile and enter a type of skill or description into the search box. This will give you a list of related skills that you can consider to use as keywords in your resume.

7. Although you may have great qualifications, spelling or grammatical errors may eliminate you from the interview process.

Think about it. People will not typically buy a dented can even if it isn't punctured.

Since many employers begin the selection process by reading your resume, consider these points before you click "send":

1. Does your resume clearly define what you have to offer accompanied by a clear objective?
2. Will the employer know what you have to offer within the first 10 seconds?
3. Does your resume give the reader the impression that you are detail oriented, organized and articulate?
4. Have you identified "quantifiable" results in your resume?
5. Are the "gotchas" minimized or addressed?—job gaps, too many jobs, over-qualifying titles, date conflicts, lack of industry keywords, general versus specifically defined skills. Consider adding a brief phrase in parentheses after your employment dates to clarify why you left a company (relocated to Arizona), (left to return to school full-time) or (position was outsourced).
6. Does your resume SELL more than it tells?

It doesn't matter how qualified you are. What matters is how well you COMMUNICATE how you can benefit an employer. You can be the best programmer in the world, but if you can't tell people why they should care, you'll be programming for free instead of getting paid for what you can do.

Stop talking about what you *DO* and start telling them what's in it for them and why they should care. Are you getting results with your current resume? If the fish aren't biting, maybe it's time to change your bait.

35

Who Are You? What Do You Do?
Who Do You Know?

Google has built social networking tools into Gmail, Google Talk and Google Reader.

If you use Google products, the company already knows your contacts, your interests and where you go on the web. Think about it. Applications are better when they know who you are. Google's focus on digital social networking should be an indicator to you that social networking needs to be a key part of your job search strategy.

Gone are the days when you just send out resumes for jobs listed on job boards and hope to get a reply. The NEW employment marketplace requires you to actively build a social network to establish RELATIONSHIPS that will lead you to your next job. Google's strategy to support interoperable, open community-driven standards will change the way you can build digital relationships using a fast evolving socially networked web. Your email address will soon become your primary on-line ID.

Connecting with people is getting easier. Access to contacts and information about others is now just a click away. Take time now to develop your contacts, set-up a system to manage your contacts and build your "personal brand" as a digital identity on the Internet. You can get Customer Relationship Management (CRM) software for free. Never forget that it's the QUALITY relationships you have that make the difference.

36

Finding Value in Social Networking

Dell has made an estimated $6 million from Twitter. Best Buy has a customer support team (TWELPFORCE) focused on Twitter.

Your personal brand is the collective impression people get not only from you and your marketing efforts, but from their interactions with you. By adding a social branding component (Twitter, LinkedIn, Facebook etc.) to your personal brand as part of your job search, you can leverage technology to promote yourself in a viral way by expanding who knows you related to on-line referrals and the search capabilities of the web. To enhance your personal brand with social branding technologies, consider incorporating these 4 ideas:

1. **Become What You Want To Be Right Now**.

   Who you are and what you want to be is as unique as a fingerprint. Act as if you are already a specialist in your area of expertise and you will become that person.

2. **Speak Your Message In Their Language**.

   Everyone in the virtual employment marketplace is talking at once so your brand has to rise above the noise. Your message, the nutshell of who you are and why people need what you have to offer, has to be short and shareable.

3. **Look The Part And Be The Part.**

Your visual identity is a symbol that carries the weight of 1000 words. It's a combination of elements you own (your name, logo, tagline, etc.) as well as elements you come to own through repeated use like writing/speaking styles and even the way you dress. Think of UPS. The color brown is part of their brand.

4. **Branding Is A Process, Not An Event.**

Peoples interests change and technology tools change. Social branding is a dynamic process requiring you to be aware of what's happening in your field. Become a student of your employment marketplace to ensure you know the latest trends and what your competitors have to offer. Study the concepts of personal AND social branding and leverage them to reach your employment goals.

37

The Magic of "Repurposing"—A Lesson from Microsoft

Near the end of 2011, Microsoft sold 960,000 Xbox 360s in 7 days, making it the best selling week in the console's history. That made the Xbox 360 one of their hottest product launches ever in terms of units sold per day! But wait! The Xbox 360 is 6 years old. The technology is essentially the same as it was when the console first came out. How can this happen?

It's the magic of repurposing.

Microsoft developed a motion sensing input device for the Xbox 360 video game console called a Kinect. It enables users to control and interact with the Xbox 360 without the need to touch a game controller using gestures and spoken commands. But the real magic came from Microsoft's repurposing of its technology tied to its Xbox console. Microsoft released a non-commercial and eventually a commercial Kinect software development kit for Windows 7 that allows .NET developers to write Kinecting apps that can be used for non-gaming applications. After selling 8 million units in 60 days, the Kinect holds the Guinness World Record of being the "fastest selling consumer electronics device. Kinect reset the console lifecycle, turning a 6 year old game machine into something that feels brand new again.

So how can you repurpose yourself?

For many job searchers, reINVENTING themselves is difficult because it requires them to radically change their skill sets.

Going back to school or starting a new business is often not an option due to immediate financial considerations.

The solution may be to rePURPOSE yourself. Take your core talents and explore ways to apply what you know to a different corporate or customer base.

Microsoft did it by expanding their gaming customer base to include software developers who took their core gaming technology and applied it to different applications.

French technologists repurposed Kinect as a gesture recognition system that can read and translate basic sign language. With more development, this could be a system for deaf or hearing-impaired users or a software tool to teach sign language.

Are the jobs you're looking for focused on what you've done in the past, or are they related to what you can do for new end-users and/or employers in a more valuable or different way? A repurposed "job search perspective" may be just the magic (mindset) you need to feel brand new again.

38

It's Not What You Know, It's What You Do.

As the Internet matures and offers almost everyone access to a worldwide body of knowledge and the capability market their products or services globally, the value of knowledge is almost becoming secondary to what you can DO with that knowledge.

Just having a degree or a certification is not enough to be perceived as talent. The successful job searcher must realize that it's not just what you know; it's what you can do with your knowledge that represents your true value to an employer.

Downsizing, outsourcing and the constant redrawing of internal organizational charts, lead to a situation in which it is less and less likely for workers to reliably turn to role-based positions for job security. These structures either no longer exist, or are themselves fading away. Being able to clearly define your area of expertise and how it can be tied to producing revenue for a company or solving a problem is the key to being competitively marketable.

The concept of "filling a position" is being replaced by "impacting the revenue". Value versus skill based employment is the new way of thinking. A good example of this perspective is highlighted by the job market for graphic designers.

Every year, thousands of graduates enter the job market armed with creative talent and a host of software skills. Yet very few survive in this very competitive business. Their demise is primarily attributed to their producing value related to time. Clients are usually billed by the project or time, so the ability to produce great results quickly is critical for success. Few can produce great designs in a short time. "Time is money" has become the common denominator to success in this time and talent based market.

Another element of talent that is often overlooked is one's ability to define their capabilities in terms of talent and value. The days of just listing your skills on a resume are a thing of the past.

Today's "power resume" needs to be defined in terms of what makes you remarkable and how your talent can solve a problem or make or save a company money.

39

It's More Than Just the Resume

Too often people spend 90% of their time on developing the perfect resume and little time on the other components of a job search. However the resume is a just a tool to open the door to building a potential employer or customer relationship. A greater payoff is found in focusing how to build a value proposition for a potential employer.

Take a look at most resumes today and you'll see a list of skills and job descriptions. Rarely do you see how one's skills translate into revenue and represent talent, as opposed to general skills common to most candidates looking for the same type of work. What you do needs to be defined as a "personal brand". Your brand is how you project yourself to the world how you ultimately influence what others think of you and how they choose to interact with you.

Stop advertising (just sending out resumes) and build relationships. We're too busy to pay attention to advertising, but we are desperate to find someone that can solve our problems. Look at your resume and ask yourself, what is it that I do that makes me stand out from the competition? How do I convey that I am remarkable compared to my professional peers.

A great example of this is the rental car business. Enterprise Rent-A-Car picks you up when you need a car—Hertz Doesn't—that makes them remarkable! It's that simple.

Another example is how Subway turned its foot-long sandwich for $5 into a top seller. By offering a simple product at a reasonable price tied to a simple dollar amount, Subway has sold over $3.8 billion dollars worth of these sandwiches in 12 months—that's more than overall product sales from Arby's and Domino's pizza combined!

Target A Niche, Not a Mass Market.

Too often, people position themselves without regard to a target market. Defining who your potential customers (employers) are PRIOR to writing your resume, is one of the key factors in getting interviews.

The "shotgun approach" of sending your resume to hundreds of employers hoping to find a match rarely works. Approaching employers with a clearly thought out offer that highlights your talent in terms of their value to an employer is what gets results. Recognize that usually your job prospects have much more to do with your local economic situation than they do with your network. The world has become a collection of unique economies in different states of maturity and with different needs related to the local labor supply. If you feel like your opportunities are limited or you have been out of work for a long time, you may need to consider moving.

Get Permission To Talk To Someone

Sending out resumes from a database list of employers is the equivalent of wearing a t-shirt that says." I'm lonely and single, will you marry me". Use referrals to get referrals so you can market yourself using relationships instead of cold-calling. Amazon is a great example of this concept. When you arrive at the Amazon homepage, you'll find not only special offers and featured products, but if you've been to Amazon.com before, you'll also find some recommendations listed for you. Amazon knows you by name and tries to be your personal shopper. Amazon's gift-giving recommendations collect data on the things you buy for other people. Although technology is the basis of their relationship with customers, the concept of knowing your customer (employer) and meeting their needs is the key to your success.

Understand the "new ROI" (Return On Influence)

Success in a talent employment market is having a "following" that knows your brand and can validate your expertise. With the new technologies offered by Twitter and LinkedIn, the employment market is now global and offers surprisingly many ways to build relationships remotely. Now you can have rich, personal interactions and find meaningful connections with others right on the Internet.

Consider writing a blog and having a personal website to differentiate yourself. Many companies have turned to the Internet to find candidates, so building a strong online presence is critical for effective networking. If you want to build your "personal brand" and enhance your job search, consider the benefits of starting a blog. You can increase networking opportunities by writing a blog focused on your field of expertise and attract other like minded professionals who may comment on your writings and maybe even contact you directly. Set up a LinkedIn profile that links to your blog so people can contact you for business or employment opportunities. Most resumes are sent by email so you can add a blog link to your resume when you apply for jobs. Your expertise and your effort in writing a blog will likely make you stand out from other job applicants.

Recognize that Attention is like Money.

People naturally filter out anything that is not meaningful to them. Listen to people. Answer their questions. Be of service without expecting anything in return and help them solve a problem. Get people's attention with an offer of help and you'll get their attention and job offers.

Consider The Way You Deliver
Your Product Or Service.

20 years ago, most hamburger restaurants were in one location run by a sole proprietor—struggling to survive. McDonald's took a different approach. Instead of just making hamburgers it became an entrepreneur. McDonald's took a step back and first figured out what the end product should look like.

They designed each element, so the bun, the onion and the patty were identical at multiple locations achieved by creating an automated process. They focused on what the customer really wanted—quality, predictability, speed and friendly service. Here the "method of delivery" made them remarkable.

How can you deliver your product or service to make yourself remarkable?

You Don't Always Need an Original Idea; Maybe You Just Need a Unique Approach.

Federal Express didn't come up with the idea of package delivery, but they did put their own unique spin on it. While attending Yale University, Fred Smith wrote a paper on the need for reliable overnight delivery and got a grade of C for his effort.

In the first 2 years of business, FedEx lost $27 million and soon the company was on the verge of bankruptcy. But the concept was right and eventually the company became a world leader in package delivery with 35 billion in annual sales and 275,000 employees. What solution can you offer than changes the way something is done to give you a competitive edge?

You Need to Develop An External AND An Internal Brand.

What do you think of yourself? If you want to position yourself as talent you have to create a mindset that you will be or are in the Top 1% of people in your field. What do you do that makes you remarkable and how can you convey that expertise to your customers (employers)? Are you passionate about what you do and do people see you as an "expert"?

Take a look at Virgin, a company that has always recognized the importance of branding. It has carefully crafted the image of being a rebel, siding with the consumer in the face of bureaucracy and monopoly. It takes an existing service or product and undercuts prices, or offers a variation on a business model.

Becoming a personal brand is the key to marketing yourself in the new job market. A carefully crafted resume that is part of a personal brand development strategy is the key to getting responses. Consider these points to position yourself as a brand:

1. Have a "brand positioning" statement at the top of your resume that is brief and highlights the attributes that make you unique.
2. Develop a network of contacts that know your brand value and are able to communicate it to others.
3. Define why your personal brand is better than your competition.
4. Have a clearly defined target audience for your brand message.
5. Develop a professional website that is specifically designed to deliver your brand message and showcase your accomplishments.
6. Make contributions to peers in your field via professional associations etc.
7. Find a mentor who can help you with your career and personal branding strategy.

Once you have crafted your resume as a marketing message to get employer (customer) interest, it's time to focus on the most critical part of the branding process—building relationships.

40

It's All About Who Knows You

Job search networking in the past was often focused on who you knew. In the new employment marketplace, it's who knows YOU. Knowledge and expertise all still important however, skills and education are now secondary to revenue impacting results.

Before the advent of social media like Facebook, LinkedIn and Twitter etc., connections and networking were targeted on who you knew.

Now with the proliferation of social media, networks can be formed more quickly by "broadcasting" the request to like-minded people who are strangers looking for someone with common interests.

Digital networking's most amazing capability is its unique ability to form social relationships in a matter of days or weeks. Social compatibility allows you to build hundreds of on-line relationships right from the comfort of your home locally and even internationally.

The most critical element in building relationships is the "FU Factor". When you make a connection, follow up. You need to follow up on connections that you feel are important. Surprisingly it's often the 2nd or 3rd call or contact that solidifies relationships. Make a habit of making lots of quick contacts with potential customers or employers on a regular basis so the connection stays alive. Without some maintenance, even the best connections can fade away and your prior efforts to build the relationship are wasted.

The Key To Building Mutually Beneficial Relationships Is About Finding Ways To Make Other People More Successful.

Keep in mind that it's not your network itself that has value for you; it's your ability to use your network to generate more relationships and get more exposure for what you have to offer.

Most people think of networking as exposure via contacts however the secret to building digital and in-person relationships is doing things for others—give value first expecting nothing in return. If you provide value to others you will increase your own. Relationships are not things that are an exchange of one thing for another—they are dynamic processes. If others succeed, you succeed—it's that simple.

Consider Forming a Master Mind Group (MMG)

The MMG concept was formally introduced by Napoleon Hill in his book "Think and Grow Rich" in the 1900's. Participants are like minded people who form a group to help someone with their goals and in turn, get help with theirs. Group members challenge each other to create and implement goals, brainstorm ideas, and support each other with total honesty and with a sincere goal to add value to what is being discussed. Your peers give you feedback, help you brainstorm new possibilities, and set up accountability structures that keep you focused and on track. You can create a community of supportive colleagues who will brainstorm together to offer you tremendous insight into ideas to improve your business just like an objective board of directors.

You are essentially the CEO of your own company as an employee or a self employed professional. Surround yourself with people that advise you in terms of helping you build your brand and expose you to business and employment opportunities. If you are a great writer but lack the technology skills to promote your work digitally, find someone with an IT background to help you. More often than not, your success will depend on building a support team of trusted advisors that can significantly enhance the building of your brand awareness.

41

Are You Involved or Committed?

The difference between involvement and commitment is like a ham and eggs breakfast: the chicken was involved but the pig was committed. Commitment is 10 times more powerful than involvement in getting the results you need. That's why you will rarely see the results you want unless you are passionate about reaching your goals. A billionaire once said that there are 3 things that you need to become successful.

1. Always be excited!
2. Always be excited!
3. Always be excited!

When you know exactly what you want and you're excited about it, the magic of desire will carry you over the many obstacles that will inevitably affect you. Just being excited about reaching your goals gives you a significant edge over others who are involved but not committed to getting what they want.

Job search and personal branding are a lot like dating related to being excited. You can tell just talking with someone if they are excited about what the future offers or they are just there for the moment. Recruiters and employers can Google your name and quickly see if you are involved or committed. Your digital identity will show them how you think and the effort you've made to brand yourself. In today's employment market, your on-line presence will more than likely determine if your resume ever gets read. It will be obvious by your on-line brand if you are just looking for work or committed to becoming an expert at what you represent as your talent.

42

When You're Green You Grow
and When You're Ripe You Rot

Being Safe is Risky. Look around you and you'll see an employment marketplace that has changed drastically within the last 2 years. Our current economic crisis has caused a global transformation from a generally time based, to an extremely results focused, job market. The world of work now offers unique opportunities for people who see innovative solutions to solving people's problems or satisfying their needs.

The key to your employment marketability will be your capability to offer well defined, marketable skills (talent), produce measurable results, and offer the capacity to make or save money for an employer or solve a problem. Look at success stories in business today and you will see how being remarkable AND cost efficient can offer you a competitive edge.

- Southwest Airlines. They fly one type of plane, the 737, and have one class of service. They sell direct to customers and go to many small airports. They cross-train their employees to do many jobs. Even the pilots help with loading the baggage. They are one of the few profitable airlines in the U.S. They are remarkable!
- A freshman at MIT designed and launched a camera 17 miles into space that took pictures of the earth for a total cost of $150. Now individuals equipped with readily available software can create remarkable things without major financial backing, a common barrier of the past that only allowed this type of innovation to be achieved by a well funded corporation.
- When you call to make an airline reservation with Jet Blue, you probably picture the agent at the other end of the line sitting in an office cubicle in a corporate call center. Their reservation agents are

people who work from home and all of them are located near Salt Lake City in Utah. By eliminating the need for a large call center and hiring home based employees, the cost savings are translated into improved revenues. Software tracks their productivity and offers management real-time metrics to keep their employee resources matched to their business needs.

- My Big Fat Greek Wedding, a romantic comedy released in 2002, became a sleeper hit despite never hitting the # 1 spot and being an independent film with a $5 million budget, ultimately grossing over $368 million worldwide.

Talent has always been in demand, however, evolving technologies and the world economy have produced an employment marketplace that puts talent as essentially the ONLY thing that is in demand now and in the foreseeable future. High level management and lower level labor jobs are becoming more scarce as companies focus on building a core talent pool tied to a more horizontal versus vertical management structure. Mid-level managers are being replaced by more centralized, and often remote web-based managers, who monitor results based on real time metrics. These changes require that you must position yourself as a competitive and talented player to remain competitive.

To see the effects of the global impact on the job market, take a look at these examples of how a product or service can become remarkable just by being more cost effective.

- Go to your local supermarket and look at the packaged shrimp. More often than not, you'll see a label indicating that the shrimp were raised in a foreign country that could be 8000 miles from the store. You can buy the shrimp for $6.99 a pound. They are caught, processed and shipped to the store with all the costs involved and they are still affordable.
- Corporate websites that cost $6000 to develop in the U.S. can be produced remotely at the same level of quality for $2000 by software developers in Russia.
- Graphic artists can bid for contracts to design logos and marketing collateral and have them printed remotely at a Kinko's available for

pick-up almost anywhere in anywhere in the world with payment made digitally through PayPal.

- Customized laptops can be ordered on line and shipped directly to customers without any interface involving a retail store.
- Lobsters in Boston can be shipped overnight packed with dry ice to any residence overnight for dinner the next day.

The Internet with its connectivity capability has opened the doors to an ecommerce business structure where competition for work and the capability to deliver products or service is now global. Think of the impact of the workers' wages in multiple global markets and how this competitively affects the availability of local jobs. Like it or not, you must choose your career and look for work factoring in the impact of global competition for what you have to offer. Since there are now more workers than jobs, the only way to be competitive is figure out a way to deliver your products or services where you can offer a compelling reason to buy from you and at a price that represents value.

43

Look Back to Look Forward

To understand where you need to go, it's important to know where you have been. Technology changes offer us a quick way to see how the past gives us clues to where the future is headed. Consider these examples.

People thought mobile computing was big when smart phones starting replacing standard cell phones. Now with mobile computing exploding, tablets are replacing desktops and the smart phone is the delivery platform for most people globally. Take a ride on public transportation and see how many people don't seem to have a car but they all seem to have a smart phone.

Think about it. Today your digital identity is either your Facebook or Google profile. If you don't have a web based identity, you are essentially invisible to the business world. Looking forward, your own personal digital brand is the key to your being found and identified as having the talent to help someone make money, save money or solve a problem. To be valuable in this changing economy, you need to position yourself to be ready to deliver talent that is competitively marketable and in demand. The key phrase is IN DEMAND. Look back 12-24 months and identify trends that you think point to where you need to be to offer a service or product that is relevant in the marketplace and ideally usable by a large group of customers (employers).

Years ago as a Boy Scout, I remember shooting a .22 rifle for the first time. After getting proficient shooting at a fixed target, I stepped up to hitting a moving target and I missed almost every time. Eventually I anticipated where the target would be by leading the moving target and figuring out when to take the shot. The new job market is a moving target. Technology requires us to think several years ahead to meet the business requirements of what we think will be in demand. Sounds complicated doesn't it?

Yet hidden within most major technology and business trends are pockets of opportunity that can offer you many years of employment. Going forward, you need to think of employment as a PROCESS not an event.

Identify a strong trend, and then decide how you can capitalize on it by offering some sort of talent related to meeting the needs of people affected by that trend. Forget about just looking for a job.

Decide now that you need a career planning STRATEGY tied to a well defined business trend where you can offer a valuable product or service. Then become an expert in what you are good at by becoming remarkable and branded as someone who is a specialist in delivering something that is in demand.

44

You Need To Compound Yourself

For most people, it's difficult for them to understand the concept of "compressing time" related to developing a career or increasing their income. Believe it or not, there is no limit to how much you can earn and how fast you can increase your income if you do it the right way.

Suppose you invested $1,000 today in a 5% savings account. In a year, that account would be worth $1,050 [$1,000 + ($1,000 x 5%)], yielding a $50 gain. In the second year, that same initial investment would be worth $1,102.50 [$1,000 + ($1,000 x 5%) + ($1,050 x 5%)], yielding a $52.50 gain. And in year three, the same $1,000 would be worth $1,157.63, yielding a $55.13 gain. By year ten, the initial $1,000 investment would be worth $1,629 and by year 25 it would be worth $3,386.

You can see that investing $1,000 today is much more valuable than investing $1,000 even a couple of years from now. To accumulate wealth, you need to understand the time value of money, the compounding effect of money and realize the importance of getting focused and started early. Career planning and income generation work the same way.

Before you decide on what you will offer as talent to an employer (customer), ask yourself, "How can I multiply the service I provide by compounding my efforts"? By having a plan to implement this concept early in your career planning, you will significantly increase the chances of your becoming an amazing success.

Consider the story of Rachel Ray.

She is a television personality, businesswoman, celebrity chef and author. She hosts the syndicated talk and lifestyle program Rachael Ray and three Food Network series, 30 Minute Meals, Rachael Ray's Tasty Travels and $40 a Day. Ray markets cookbooks based on the 30 Minute Meal concept, and launched a magazine, Every Day with Rachael Ray. Forbes magazine reported that a few years ago, Ray earned about $6 million annually from her books and television shows.

In 1995 Rachel moved to New York City. One of her first jobs there was at the candy counter at Macy's, where she eventually managed the fresh foods department. Moving back to upstate New York, Ray managed Mister Brown's Pub at The Sagamore, a hotel on Lake George. From there, she became a buyer at Cowan & Lobel, a gourmet market in Albany.

Eventually she ended up teaching a course where she demonstrated how to make meals in less than 30 minutes. With the success of her "30 Minute Meals" classes, WRGB a CBS TV affiliate, asked her to appear in a weekly segment on their newscasts. This, along with a public radio appearance and the publication of her first book, led to a Today show spot and her first Food Network contract in 2001. Rachel took her skills as a cook and compounded her efforts by reaching out to large groups of people with her books and television shows. Her 30 Minute Meals cooking classes took her from the candy counter at Macy's to earning $6 million a year!

Look carefully at what happened to Rachel. She became remarkable by focusing on something she was passionate about and over time, expanded her services and products to entertain and help lots of people.

45

See the Forest and the Trees

Too often we focus on today's issues and forget about where we are going long term. It's very easy to get caught up in the details of a situation or where we are in our career.

Recognize that your self-image and what you know about yourself primarily comes from feedback from other people. That's why the quickest way to discovering your remarkability in the employment market is to get feedback about your ideas and planning from people who will honestly offer you varying perspectives on what you plan to do. Getting feedback from others is the key to seeing where you are now and if your plans for the future make sense.

A micro AND macro approach to developing your personal brand needs to evolve from feedback from others so your emotional commitment to what you are pursuing doesn't distort the reality of your circumstances. A simple way to ensure that you combine both perspectives is to decide what you want and then build a bridge to get it. Have the end in sight and work backwards to develop the infrastructure you need to get what you want. Too many people look for work by surveying what's available instead of going after what they want.

Pay particular attention to this concept as it relates to having a PLAN that is an on-going process not just an EVENT. Clear goals are essential to the success of a business and building your career.

If you don't take the time to know exactly what it is you're trying to accomplish, then you're destined to spend your life helping other people achieving their goals instead of your own. You may make some money, and you may have some interesting jobs, but the end result will not resemble anything you ever made a conscious decision to build. Setting clear goals is not a passive act. It doesn't happen automatically. You must take direct conscious action in order to make it happen.

You are either moving towards your goals, or you're moving away from them. It can be as simple as picking a point in the future, a year from now or three years from now, and spend a few hours writing out a clear description of where you want to be at that time.

By deciding exactly what you want, writing it down, and reviewing it on a daily basis, you bring your goals into reality with the power of your focus.

46

Changing the Problem

In the early days of NASA's attempt to explore space they faced a seemingly impossible problem. How could they make a material that could stand up to the heat generated by the re-entry of a spacecraft? They had to find a material that would not melt. Countless trials ended in failure because the heat was so intense.

They solved that problem by focusing on finding a material that would melt. The solution was to add a shell that would melt off as the craft re-entered the earth's atmosphere.

If you can't find a solution, maybe you need to change the problem. In the old world of work, the solution was to find a job where you could develop a career and work your way into management. You expected an average annual salary increase of 4-5% and earned accumulating weeks of vacation based on your years of service to a company.

In the new status quo, multiple employers are becoming the norm and the new solution is to develop several streams of income, ideally with one involving a residual income. Your problem is NOT to get a job; it's to DO a job for multiple customers (employers).

Your NEW challenge (problem) is to get multiple employers (customers) to provide you a diversified stream of income based on your delivery of solutions that help them make money, save money or solve a problem. Start using this mindset and your job search will take a different perspective and offer you far more employment security than most people have ever had. Employment security used to come from a company, now it needs to come from YOU and the talent you offer. Now more than ever, you need to focus on what you're doing AND where you are going. Your solution is to change the problem and come up with a new solution. Changing the problem may be as simple as focusing on these 4 things.

1. Who you know.
2. Who knows YOU?
3. What talent represents your personal brand?
4. The quality of your relationships.

How many people would work for Richard Branson, Chairman of the Virgin Group, for 90 days without pay, just to get insights into improving their personal brand?

Focus on the results you can produce, build a reputation as an expert, and establish a network of quality relationships and watch your market value and income increase automatically.

47

Start by Stopping

Sometimes it's what you STOP doing that determines if you will reach your goals. You need to form new habits to break free of activities that distract you from accomplishing what you need to do to get ahead.

Avoid "reactionary work" and start focusing on what you can do each day to reach your goals. You can easily spend your entire day just responding to email, texts, voicemails and tweets and never find time to work on what really matters. Work with a focus on your goals instead of reacting to events. If you are spending 3 hours a day in unproductive activities, that amounts to 15 hours per 5-day-work-week or 60 hours per month. What could you have done in those 60 hours to help you complete your current job? How would you use the 60 hours to increase your bottom line?

Figure out what distracts you. Identify what is blocking your ability to keep your attention on what needs your attention. A simple yet powerful way to keep yourself on track is "The Top 6."

Set up a document on your computer that lists the Top 6 things you need to accomplish related to your GOALS not daily tasks. Look at it when you get started in the morning and just before you go to bed at night. If you don't accomplish your #1 goal during the day, move it to the top the next day. Seeing this list will help you keep focused during the day and embed your subconscious mind with your goals while you sleep at night. A magical thing will happen if you do this for 30 days. It will become a habit.

Becoming goal oriented versus task oriented is what will help you stop doing things that are more distractions than productive actions. Ask yourself, "What are 6 things that if I accomplish them, will make the most difference in the quality of my life?" Thinking about them each day will super charge your brain to act like a magnet to draw thoughts and actions into your life that will help you reach your goals. Remember the saying, "out of sight out of mind? If you want to lose 15 pounds, and each day you see your weight on a spreadsheet with a chart that shows your progress, you are far more likely to achieve your goal. Think about your goals each day and see how you become magically more productive and motivated when you focus on your goals instead of just reacting to non-productive tasks.

48

Automate

Have you ever stopped to consider that the most productive use of your time has the same relative cost as the least productive use of your time? Essentially each day you only have 24 hours to use and it can be productive or unproductive.

To become remarkable you must increase the VALUE of your time by leveraging your efficiency or delegating tasks so you can focus on what you do best. Software alone does not improve productivity. In order to maximize your efficiency, you need to identify what you do most often during a typical day that is critical to reaching your goals and then search for a technology that can enhance the efficiency of those activities.

Consider Apple's Siri-powered voice command speech-to-text technology. Think about the time you use to transcribe an email or text message with your fingers and thumbs. Contrast that to just speaking and having your message magically appear on your phone or a computer document. In a week's time, think of how much more productive you can be just by having this technology.

Automation can also help you focus on building relationships which are key to developing your personal brand. Take a look at Xobni for Outlook. It finds all the people you know through your emails, SMS messages and phone calls, and automatically creates a rich profile for them. Each profile includes their photo, signature information, and the messages you've exchanged, as well as their updates from Facebook, Twitter and LinkedIn. It turns your Outlook into a client relationship management (CRM) tool and offers an instant analysis of who emails you the most and what time of the day you get most of your emails.

These are just 2 examples of software that can change unproductive time into productive time. Essentially you need to periodically assess your "capacity to deliver" whatever it is that makes you remarkable. The key word to note is periodically. Set aside time (actually schedule) time to research new technologies with the mindset of improving your productivity. Think of it as continuing education to maintain an awareness of best practices in your field of work.

49

The Person in the Mirror

For most people, getting through each day convinces them that they are doing the right thing and their life will take its natural course. To become remarkable you need to know EXACTLY where you are in your life as it relates to your goals.

Since few people have WRITTEN goals, they probably never realize that they are unlikely to end up where they want to be. There's a simple solution to this problem. Prepare a document that describes where you are with your life right now. Make sure it's digital so you can update it easily. Knowing where you are is the first step in moving forward to make the changes to become what you want to be. Your goal is to measure what matters. Consider including these items:

1. Top 3 Specific Marketable Skills (Things that would make you valuable to an employer)
2. What makes you remarkable?
3. Greatest Weakness(related to your business capabilities)
4. 6 goals directly tied to where you want to be in 3 years
5. Current Net Worth (Subtract your assets from your liabilities)
6. Net Worth a year ago
7. Net Worth 2 years ago
8. What do you need to STOP doing to become more productive?
9. Your health—height/weight/last comprehensive exam/weight 12 months ago
10. If you could change one thing in your life that would ensure you reaching your goals, what would it be?

Keep in mind that you are always moving ahead or falling behind. It's impossible to stay the same person you are today. Your capacity to deliver value requires that you reinvent or revitalize yourself to keep up with technology, the changing employment marketplace and what you can offer that is in demand.

50

Invisible to Remarkable

With the constant evolution of the capabilities of the Internet and its power to allow you to reach a global market, your connectivity to the world-wide-web is the gift of a life-time. Now more than ever, YOU have the power to control your own economic security and the quality of your life by focusing on building a remarkable personal brand (talent). We live in an era where providing products and services that truly stand out are no longer optional. You need to become your own personal brand. It's the only way to survive in the new employment marketplace where most of us will DO a job versus HAVE a job.

But being remarkable today also requires loyal fans that spread the word about the quality and excellence of your product or service.

Since your income will almost always be in direct proportion to the number of people you serve, remarkability AND relationships are 2 things you must have for your employment and economic security going forward.

Here's where the Internet has opened the door for you to build relationships with virtually anyone that has an Internet connection. Look around you and you'll see that your age, credit access, education and how you look more often than not, have little to do with success. Remarkability, relationships, talent and a burning desire to succeed will make you a winner. The person you will be in 4 years will primarily be determined by (1) the people you hang around with, (2) your capability to use technology as a business tool, (3) your direct action to reach predetermined measurable goals and (4) what you read.

Becoming a personal brand won't happen overnight but it will happen if you remind yourself daily that you become what you think about most often and take action to reach your goals.

A few years ago I finished a gym workout and went back to the locker room where I saw a piece of paper posted on the wall. It read, "Change your thoughts, to change your world". After a bit of self reflection, I realized that this simple insight was the key to reinventing myself and the "secret ingredient" to help others reach their goals.

In December, 2011, Comic Louis C.K. released his 4th full-length special, Live at the Beacon Theater. It was produced independently and directed by C.K., but unlike his earlier work, it was distributed only digitally on the comedian's website, without using printed or broadcast media. In 10 days, his website generated over $1,000,000 dollars selling over 220,000 copies for $5 each.

Now it's your turn to make it happen.

Talent isn't the next big thing, it's the only thing.

If you aren't **Remarkable**, you're invisible.